MEMORANDA

RELATIVE TO

THE LINES

THROWN UP TO COVER LISBON

IN 1810

COLONEL JOHN T. JONES, R.E.

The Naval & Military Press Ltd

published in association with

FIREPOWER
The Royal Artillery Museum
Woolwich

Published by
The Naval & Military Press Ltd
Unit 10 Ridgewood Industrial Park,
Uckfield, East Sussex,
TN22 5QE England
Tel: +44 (0) 1825 749494
Fax: +44 (0) 1825 765701
www.naval-military-press.com

in association with

FIREPOWER
The Royal Artillery Museum, Woolwich
www.firepower.org.uk

In reprinting in facsimile from the original, any imperfections are inevitably reproduced and the quality may fall short of modern type and cartographic standards.

PREFACE.

The following Memoranda contain a portion of the ten sheets which the author deemed it right to withdraw from the second edition of the "Journals of Sieges," in consequence of a military force being sent to Lisbon at the moment of their being printed.

These Memoranda were originally drawn up with the view of making known to those who had not the opportunity of personal inspection, the nature and extent of the defences created to cover Lisbon. They are now distributed with the same view; and if they prove useful to any brother officer seeking professional information, the writer will consider himself well repaid for the trouble of extracting them from his notes.

Il est des militaires qui demandent à quoi servent les places fortes, les camps retranchés, l'art de l'ingenieur; nous leurs demanderons à notre tour comment il est possible de maneuvrer avec des forces inferieures ou égales sans le secour des positions, des fortifications et de tous les moyens supplementaires de l'art.—*Conversations de Napoleon, par Montholon.*

CHAPTER I.

THE retrenched positions covering Lisbon, known under the denomination of the Lines of Torres Vedras, have gained so much celebrity, as having formed the barrier from which the tide of French conquest first receded, and moreover possess so many peculiarities of defence, and are so free from the objections usually urged against lines, that some observations on their nature, construction, and mode of occupation, can scarcely fail to be interesting to professional and other officers seeking military information; and happily, since the first edition of this work was penned, in 1813, the affairs of Europe have so changed as to admit of some degree of descriptive detail being without impropriety substituted for the former eulogium of the general merit of the lines.

The determination to commence these works may be dated from the battle of Talavera. The offensive movements which led to that action having put to the test the value of Spanish co-operation, and having fully demonstrated the utter inefficiency of their armies, from want of organization, want of discipline and skilful officers, it became apparent to the Duke of Wellington that the contest would, in the next campaign, devolve on the small body of veteran British and newly raised Portugueze troops under his command, and a defensive system of warfare ensue. To prepare for a final struggle was thenceforward the great object of consideration; and as the hope of successfully defending an extended and open frontier, like that of Portugal, against a very superior and highly skilful enemy, could scarcely be entertained, it was decided to seek out some position in the lower part of Estramadura, not liable to be turned or passed, and having an assured communication with the sea, which should command all the approaches to Lisbon, and which position, being retrenched in the strongest manner, would offer a point of concentration for the whole of the defensive forces of Portugal, army, militia, irregulars, &c. where they might, in conjunction with the British, be victualled and supplied with ammunition for any period of time, whilst occupying a most favourable field for deciding the fate of the capital and the kingdom in a general action.

With these views, whilst the army was cantoned on the Guadiana, Lord Wellington, in the month of October, 1809, attended by his quarter-master-general, Colonel Murray, and his chief engineer, Lieutenant-Colonel Fletcher, made a personal reconnoissance of the country in front of Lisbon, and judging the scheme practicable by means of a chain of fortified posts to extend across the peninsula, directed the officers of engineers to examine and minutely delineate the various strong features of ground between the sea and the Tagus, on a breadth of several miles, in order to enable him to decide on the most eligible line of defence whenever he should deem the moment arrived for commencing the work. In the meanwhile the defences of Fort St. Julian at the mouth of the Tagus were to be extended to cover and ensure a communication with the fleet; and ground was to be occupied as retrenched posts or positions at Castanheira, Monte Agraça, and Torres Vedras, to support the manœuvres of the army while retiring on the meditated line, or place of embarkation. (1)

These labours proceeded uninterruptedly till the commencement of February, 1810, when, the preparations of the French for the conquest of Portugal having assumed a decided character, Lord Wellington, during the march of his army from the Guadiana to the Coa, revisited

Lisbon to give final orders respecting the works to be erected for its protection. A few days were sufficient to ride over and decide on the ranges of hills convertible to his views; and having fixed the principal points and grand outline of his defensive system, he rejoined his army on the frontier, leaving the plan, trace, and execution of the works to Lieut.-Colonel Fletcher, whose sound military knowledge and indefatigable zeal were pledges for the details being worthy of the design.

At this time it was presumed that the invading army would be nearly double the strength of the defensive force, and equal to manœuvre, in two formidable bodies, on the right and left of the Tagus, so as to throw back their opponents hastily on Lisbon; or, if parried in strategy, likely to attempt wearing them out by a succession of sanguinary combats. Expectation of a successful resistance was therefore very doubtingly entertained, and the object of primary interest and attention was to secure places for re-embarking the army in case of disaster, or if the enemy should advance before the lines could be rendered of sufficient strength to make it prudent to occupy them. The next consideration was to establish such strong enclosed works to block up the passes as should enable indifferent troops to delay or check a hostile column, in its endeavours to interrupt the retrograde manœuvres of the regular army; and these paramount objects being attained, every effort was to be used to strenghten the selected ranges of hills to the utmost that time would admit.

From the rocky nature of the coast of Portugal, there are very few spots favourable for maritime communication; and in the space to be covered by the projected lines, only one suitable point could be found, being a small bay, not two hundred yards in length, and very partially sheltered from the ocean by Fort St. Julian at the mouth of the Tagus; and even at that spot, at intervals, such a sea rolls in for days together that no boat can with safety approach the shore.*

The works to cover an embarkation were therefore to be traced of a threefold nature: first, to form a position of such extent that the

* Even in the advanced season, between the end of April and middle of June, 1810, at the large fishing town of Ericeira, such a surf prevailed that the boats could not be launched for a single morning.

In 1811, four jetties, to cover the place of embarkation at St. Julian, were constucted by Captain Holloway, at an expense of £15,000, which, notwithstanding every local and nautical opinion being unfavourable to their stability, resisted the most furious gales of wind throughout the war, and rendered an embarkation practicable in all seasons and weather.

whole army might sustain itself and protect its artillery and stores, during any period of bad weather which might retard the commencement of the embarkation; secondly, with an enclosed work within the principal trace, of such size and strength as might admit of diminished numbers defending themselves, should a gale of wind come on after one portion of the troops had been embarked; or should the army have met with such severe loss on its retreat, previously to reaching the point of embarkation, as to preclude the possibility of occupying the outer line; and lastly, with a small post on the shore sufficiently strong to protect the rear guard, and ensure its safe embarkation.

The first object was obtained by means of a line of detached redoubts and intermediate defences, appuying its right on the Tagus, near Fort das Maias, and its left on the ocean behind the canal at the little fort or tower of Junquiera. The works of this exterior line commanded the town of Oeyras, and included within their trace, the contour of which measured 3,000 yards, the whole promontory, at the extremity of which stands Fort St. Julian. The second was effected by the construction of a large irregular enclosed work, occupying the summit of the height immediately in front of Fort St. Julian. The last object was found in Fort St. Julian itself, which, from its extravagantly high scarps and deep ditches, can never be successfully assaulted against the slightest opposition.

As a secondary point of embarkation, and looking to the probability of a series of operations terminating on the left of the Tagus, a line of works was to be thrown up at Setuval, to cover the right bank of that harbour, and keep open its communication with the sea. These works were to be formed partly of a connected trace and partly of detached redoubts, their right being closely supported by Fort St. Phillippe, and their left resting on a scarped cliff. The front of defence rather exceeded 1,500 yards, and, besides occupying the ground most favourable for the erection of batteries to annoy the transports, formed, with Fort St. Phillippe, a strong post, in which a division might maintain itself during the embarkation of the main-body of the army, and ultimately effect its retreat by the sacrifice of a small rear guard in the Fort.

The principal line of defence, denominated subsequently the second line, was formed on the knowledge that only four great paved roads lead to Lisbon, between the sea and the Tagus, below the point where that river from its encreased depth and breadth becomes, in a military sense, impassable to an army—that three of those roads, at nearly parallel points, pass over or between heights of extraordinary strength, viz. at the passes of Mafra, Montachique, and Bucellas, and that the fourth, bordering on the Tagus where the ground is less bold, passes under a strong range of heights at Alhandra, nearly two leagues in advance of the right of the above mentioned line of passes; and further, that the country between the paved roads being hilly and broken could not, without the utmost delay and difficulty, be crossed at any part by an army with its artillery. It was proposed to block up the passes with formidable works, and to support their defence by forming the different ranges of heights between them into one uniformly strong line, so as to ensure a connected barrier across the peninsula, which an invader must force through by a front attack before he could reach Lisbon.

Nature had done much in aid of this design: commencing on the left from the sea at the hamlet of Ribamar, in front of Ericeira, and following up the course of the little river St. Lorenzo to Cacheca, adjoining the pass of Mafra, a distance of seven miles, a deep, rugged, and in many parts impracticable, ravine leaves scarcely a favourable point for a battalion to advance in column. This flank therefore presents no inducement whatever for an invader to select it for his principal line of operations, and it was considered that, in the first instance, the destruction of the peasants' tracks, and establishing artillery in secure enclosed works, 88 to 94, on the projecting points, to flank the most accessible part of the ascent, would be sufficient to enable a small corps of observation to secure this portion of the line till reinforced.

The pass of Mafra was strengthened with peculiar care, and considerable labour; for although the main ascent, viewed as an isolated feature, possesses great strength, there is much ground on its right enclosed with a wall as a royal park (tapada), the features of which are but very moderately bold; and moreover two roads run nearly parallel to the northern and southern boundaries of the tapada, which offer great facilities to an enemy to manœuvre and carry the pass by a flank attack. The main ascent being rendered secure by means of redoubts and emplacements for artillery, so disposed as to enfilade the road and concentrate their fire upon points of it where deep and broad cuts, and other artificial obstructions, were marked out to be formed at the required moment, the principal labour was directed to secure the flanks of the pass. The wall of the tapada, or royal park, had a banquette added to its interior, and efficient flanks were created along its front, either raised for field-pieces or loop-holed for musketry; and a chain of redoubts, 74 to 77, was thrown up on the most commanding points within the enclosure, to sweep the ravines and interdict the passage along the road in its rear. Further, each feature of the ground overlooking the approach to the tapada was occupied by a redoubt, well furnished with a powerful and commanding artillery, 62, 63, 64. The strong heights above Gradil, called the Serra de Chypre, so situated on the road from Torres Vedras as equally to obstruct the march of a column by the main pass of Mafra and the collateral branches on the left of Morugueira, was also strengthened to the utmost, by redoubts 78 to 81.

A little in rear, and to the left of the village of Morugueira, works were established, 82, 83 and 84, for the defence of the minor pass by Cacheca, and as a communicating link of the chain between Mafra and the left extremity of the line.

Further, to guard against these important points being turned with artillery on their left, and that the security of the strong corps likely to be allotted for the defence of the main pass of Mafra should not be altogether dependent on a successful defence of the extensive line of the ravine between Morugueira and Ribamar, a retired post was established at Carvoiera, on the left of the Chilleros valley, 96 and 97, to command the only coast road from Ericeira to Cintra, St. Julian's and Lisbon, in its descent of the opposite bank of the valley; and that road where most under fire of the redoubts was to be mined for destruction. No. 95, situated on a strong feature of ground on the right of the valley, co-operated in these objects.

Lastly, the town of Mafra itself was formed into a defensive post towards Ericeira, and was covered on that side by a chain of works, 85, 86, 87, blocking up the only lateral approaches practicable for artillery.

The next object of attention was the pass of Cabeça-de-Montachique. The heights forming the immediate flanks of that pass being naturally as strong and favourable for defence as can be desired, little labour was bestowed on them, and the principal consideration was to block up the road. For this purpose twenty-five pieces of artillery were secured in redoubts (No: 52 to 61 inclusive), situated on strong features, mostly in advance of the principal range of heights to the right and left of the great paved communication from Torres Vedras and from Sobral through Zibriera, which, completely enfilading a considerable length of the approach, were considered to render a direct attack along the road hazardous in the extreme. This disposition of the redoubts was caused by the advanced features of the ground intimately connecting with each other, and being deemed to form a chain of posts collectively stronger than the main features of the pass. It is, however, an example of fortifying to be followed with great caution, it being contrary to all just principles of defence, to extend a chain of small posts in advance of a main feature—that is, to court an action in detail, and is utterly inadmissible in the defence of a pass, wherever the approach is such that an enemy can act off the great road.

The defensive features of the country, from the pass of Mafra to that of Cabeça-de-Montachique, are less distinctly marked than along any other portion of the line; but the hills, though not continuous or precipitous, are high, steep and salient, affording the means of covering a parallel road which connects the two passes. These hills were occupied by isolated redoubts, 62 to 73, overlooking the difficult country in their front, commanding every approach to the lateral road, and securing that communication to the defenders—they were consequently both outposts and guards to a chain of rather formidable heights in rear of the road; and which heights thus covered were considered to offer a favourable field of action, should an enemy think it worth while to attack a re-entering line, from whence only one indifferent road for artillery exists to facilitate his further movement, and against which artillery could only be brought by previously forcing the works near Gradil (Serra de Chypre), or the advanced defences of the pass of Montachique.

From Montachique to the pass of Bucellas the heights are of a nature to preclude the necessity of works, except for the purpose of blocking up a road for cavalry, and perhaps cars, over the ridge at Freixal, which was effected by retrenchments, 49, 50, 51.

The pass of Bucellas is of the strongest description, the road running between two high and steep mountains, through an opening of only a few hundred yards: the defence of the pass consequently hinged on the troops maintaining possession of the flanks of the mountains, and all an engineer could do was to establish secure emplacements for artillery to enfilade the pass, to mine the bridge at its entrance for destruction, and create other obstructions on the road to detain the advancing columns under their fire. The approach was thus guarded by works, 43 to 47, and in case of disaster 45 was intended to cover the retreat of the defenders.

From the pass of Bucellas towards the Tagus,

the Serra de Serves, a high and extremely difficult ridge with scarcely any break, occupies a front exceeding two miles to the road, which crosses it from Villa de Rey. Its right flank then overlooks and gradually falls on the low ground bounding the Tagus. This space of two miles and a half between the right of the mountain and the river, presented full scope for art and labour, and advantage was taken of every feature of the ground to give it strength. Works were multiplied along its centre, No. 34 to 39, in front of Via Longa, and also on the bluff extremity of the Serra de Serves, above Portella, 40, 41, and 42, forming its left flank. Its right flank, resting on the Tagus and closed by a strong redoubt, No. 33, it was proposed further to secure by deep and broad cuts through the salt-pans in its front, made in a direction to be enfiladed by the fire of gun-boats; but notwithstanding all the labour thus bestowed on this portion of the line, it was confessedly much the weakest, and great dependence was placed on the aid it would derive from a peculiar chain of strong heights, forming almost an isolated feature, about five miles in its front, at Alhandra. These heights it was proposed to dispute with an advanced corps, and works, 1 to 4, were established to enfilade the main road, flank the low ground, and equalize the strength of the front; and redoubts, 5, 7, 8, were thrown up as impediments to the position being turned with artillery.

The above mentioned features of country (occupying 22 miles of front) thus connected and strengthened with 59 redoubts, mounting 232 pieces of artillery, and requiring 17,500 men for their garrisons, formed the principal line of defence across the peninsula, and fulfilled all the conditions sought for in a position to cover Lisbon. The works which, under the first view of the army retiring into Estramadura, had been thrown up on the heights of Torres Vedras and Monte Agraça, 14 to 17, and 20 to 27, served as valuable outposts to this defensive line, from six to nine miles in its front, blocking up the principal approaches, and assuring the troops time to take up their ground and occupy the new defences before they could be attacked in force. These advanced works were completely isolated posts, except that the country on the left of Torres Vedras being open, and offering an inviting facility to an enemy to turn that defile and the works for its defence, the passage of the little river Zizandra was guarded or rather watched by three redoubts established on its left bank at St. Pedro de Cadeira, and in rear of Ponte de Rol, 30, 31, and 32; and with the same view, as respects Monte Agraça, redoubts 9 to 13 were thrown up in the pass of Arruda.

Two strong isolated features of ground which command the main roads at the intermediate points of Ajuda and Enxara dos Cavalleiros were also retrenched, Nos. 18 and 19—28 and 29, as additional impediments to the rapid advance of an enemy on the principal line.

Signal posts for the purpose of instant communication between these various detached works, and generally along the whole front of defence, were established on the points best uniting an extensive view with perfect security.

Lisbon, the prize to be disputed, situated twelve miles in rear of Via Longa, fifteen miles in rear of the pass of Bucellas, twelve in rear of the pass of Montachique, and twenty-three in rear of the pass of Mafra, is of great size, and advantageously placed for defence and subsistence on the right bank of the Tagus. Its buildings are of such an incombustible nature as to render bombardment almost harmless; and the approaches being generally narrow and sunken, and flanked by stone houses having the doors and windows secured with iron gratings, and other defensive expedients, render the suburbs peculiarly susceptible of an irregular defence. It was not therefore deemed necessary to fortify the enceinte, but the Portugueze were encouraged to erect barriers and traverses at the several entries, to create interior posts, to mount guns on the castle, the Peña convent, and other domineering and strong points; and by their exertions the city was expected to be placed altogether beyond a coup-de-main when occupied by such forces as it was intended at the moment of danger to throw into it.

St. Julian, the point of embarkation in the event of defeat or discomfiture, is situated twenty-four miles in rear of Carvoiera, and twenty-seven miles in rear of the pass of Mafra; the high road to it from the other passes being through Lisbon, though it may be reached from either of them by tolerable cross-country communications without passing through that city.

These extensive works were pressed forward by Lieut.-Colonel Fletcher and his officers with the greatest zeal and ardour, and they were liberally supplied with means. A detachment of infantry was selected to act as overseers, directors, and artificers; two regiments of Portugueze militia were allotted as pioneers, the peasantry of the surrounding districts were put into requisition as labourers, and no petty cavils about official forms of expenditure were allowed to impede the supply of materials and stores. (2)

Napoleon had proclaimed early in the year, with more than his usual arrogance, that he was collecting a force of 110,000 invincibles on the frontiers of Portugal to drive the English out of the Peninsula; and it was naturally concluded that he would act at least with his wonted celerity and enterprize—that he would push forward to the main object, regardless of isolated fortresses, and strike a final blow before means of resistance could be matured.

The several works of the lines were in consequence thrown up in haste, and of a construction requiring the least labour, compatible with a certain degree of strength: the redoubts were generally made of a field profile of a size to require from 150 to 250 and 300 men for their defence, and were armed, according to the importance of their fire, with three, four, five, or six pieces of artillery.

The main works at Torres Vedras, Monte Agraça above Sobral, and Oeyras, being considered independent forts, or rather species of petty fortresses, were made larger and stronger than the works at other places; particularly those of Torres Vedras, which blocking up the most direct road to the point of embarkation, and being moreover on the spot of former enterprises, were regarded with peculiar jealousy: they were of a trace to be tolerably flanked, and of a magnitude to require a garrison of 2,200 men with 40 pieces of cannon, independently of the number required to guard the lines of communication with the convent of St. Joa, and the castle in the town, which latter were formed into good posts, Nos. 25 and 27, and mounted with seven pieces of artillery.

The main work on Monte Agraça, which was made roomy and spacious, required a garrison of nearly 1,000 men, and was armed with 25 pieces of ordnance; it was, however, very imperfectly flanked, and the profile was almost the same as that of the small redoubts. In advance of this main work, at various points of the ridge, the dependent redoubts, 15, 16, 17, mounting 19 guns, and requiring above 1,000 men for their defence, (the whole being considered to form only one post, occupying the summit of Monte Agraça,) were thrown up to flank and see the ascent. The inclosed work on the height between Oeyras and St. Julian's was sufficiently flanked, and of a magnitude to require a garrison of 1;340 men, and on it and its dependent redoubts and batteries above 50 pieces of ordnance were mounted.

The above-mentioned three principal works were furnished with 160 rounds of ammunition per gun, thirty of which were grape, and 200 hand grenades: the other redoubts were supplied with 60 rounds per gun, eight of which were grape shot, and from 12 to 16 hand grenades each.

The artillery mounted in the several works were 12, 9, or 6 prs. with two or three $5\frac{1}{2}$ inch field howitzers in the larger forts; they were all Portugueze iron ordnance, on carriages of a most primitive construction, with such low trucks as to be perfectly immoveable over broken ground, and consequently not to be immediately rendered useful to an enemy on carrying a redoubt. The artillery of every work, being mounted with the view to guard some fixed object, fired through embrazures.

It has been stated that the works of St. Julian,* Monte Argraça,† and Torres Vedras,‡ were the first commenced in the autumn of 1809, as isolated points, with the view of having some defence prepared for the army, should the invaders instantly advance as they threatened. The works for the defence of the passes were next undertaken,§ and ultimately, in the spring of 1810, the whole were in progress. With

* On the 3d November, by Capt. Wedekind.

† On the 4th ditto, by Capt. Williams.

‡ On the 8th ditto, by Capt. Mulcaster.

§ Viz. Mafra, on the 17th Feb. by Capt. Ross;—Ericeira and Carvoiera, 19th Feb. by Lieut. R. Jones;—Montachique do. Capt. Mulcaster;—Via Longa, 24th Feb. Lieut. Stanway;—Arruda, 17th March, Lieut. Forster;—Ponte do Rol, 26th March, Lieut. Thomson.

the same feeling the works at St. Julian's were originally confined to the heights between the fort and the town of Oeyras: in the spring, and early in the summer of 1810, the advanced line of redoubts 103, 104, 105, 106, 107, 108,* was thrown up; and in the autumn, the exterior points were occupied, and the advanced defences completed.†

Such was the original plan and construction of the lines which, when nearly brought to the degree of perfection that the aspect of affairs seemed to admit, were given over to the charge of Captain John T. Jones, by Lieut.-Colonel Fletcher, on the 6th July, 1810; and the advance of the invaders being momentarily expected, himself hastened to the scene of active operations on the Coa.‡

* Principally by Capt. Squire.

† It will be seen from the above dates that, except at Monte Agraça, a point quite out of the beaten track, and almost unknown to the British, the works of Torres Vedras were undertaken three months before any other part of the lines, which accidental circumstance, added to the previous celebrity of the pass, caused their name to be given to the whole system of defence.

‡ "COMMANDING ROYAL ENGINEERS' ORDERS.

"*Mafra, 6th July*, 1810.

"As Lieut.-Colonel Fletcher, Captains Chapman, Squire, and Goldfinch are about to join the army, Capt. Jones will be left in the immediate command and superintendence of all works

It would appear that, soon after Col. Fletcher's arrival at Lord Wellington's head-quarters, the proposed mode of occupying the lines underwent consideration, and some change was contemplated, (probably in consequence of the invaders engaging in the siege of Almeida, which gave expectation of the rains commencing previously to the final struggle, which, as will be hereafter shown, would materially change the relative strength of some portions of the coun-

and duties connected with the Engineer Department in this part of Portugal, and he is therefore to be obeyed accordingly.

(Signed,) R. FLETCHER,
Lieut.-Colonel Commanding Engineer."

Memorandum of officers left under Capt. Jones's orders.

Captain Holloway,
Williams,
Dickenson.
Lieut. Stanway,
Thomson,
Forster,
Trench,
Piper,
Tapp,
Reid,
Hulme.
Captain Wedekind, } King's German Legion.
Lieut. Meinecke, }
Lorenzo Homen, }
Sousa, } Portugueze Service.
Britto, }

try,) for, on the 17th July, orders were issued to strengthen, as far as possible, the right flank of the advanced ground, on which the posts of Torres Vedras and Monte Agraça had been established, and to throw up additional works for the further security and strength of its left flank; also to add various exterior defences to the position, covering the place of embarkation on the right of the Tagus.

In consequence of these orders, renewed exertions were made on the lines, and as many workmen as could be advantageously employed were collected at each point to be strengthened. The young officers now, for the first time, placed in charge of extensive districts, exerted themselves with a zeal which knew no limits, and every where throughout the lines a spirit of honourable emulation proved highly advantageous to the progress of the work.

On the right the musketry trench No. 1, across the marsh between the Tagus and the heights of Alhandra, and the trench No. 2, ascending from the marsh to the summit of the heights, were converted into strong lines; and the left of the former was so far thrown back as to admit of the ground in its front being generally and closely flanked by retired batteries, which were excavated in the flank of the mountain.—These batteries were of a very powerful nature, and being completely covered from all ground in their front, could not be cannonaded, or even seen by an enemy, till almost on the glacis of the defences across the low ground, and consequently rendered any effort to force that line utterly hopeless.

From the right of the mountain of Alhandra, two miles of front were, as a field position, rendered strong to an excess, for along the face of the mountain, near its summit, a scarp almost perpendicular, from 15 to 18 feet in depth, was cut or blasted; every part of which was closely flanked by a covered musketry fire, and generally flanked by artillery, secured in inclosed works constructed on the salient points of the heights—all these flanking works being seen, and plunged into by larger and stronger redoubts, situated on commanding interior peaks of the mountain, 114 to 120.*

At this time, Alhandra being considered an advanced position to the line of Via Longa, in order to prevent its being turned on its left, the heights above Calhandrix, at a spot where they

* Could it have been foreseen in July, that time would have been allowed by the invaders for carrying the scarps and other defences of Alhandra to the degree of strength they ultimately attained before the army entered the lines, the flanking guns on the salient points of the scarped ridge would have been placed in open batteries instead of strong redoubts.

narrow to a rocky ridge, not exceeding six hundred yards in breadth, were, on the representations of the executive officer, ordered to be occupied with a chain of redoubts supporting each other. Fifteen hundred men commenced these works, 121, 122, 123, and 124, on the 6th September, and miners being at the same time employed to scarp the flanks of the ridge, it soon formed a strong detached position across the only range of heights over which artillery could travel to turn Alhandra.

In order to block up the valley between the heights of Alhandra and Calhandrix, and to connect the defence of those positions, a strong abattis, with a covered communication in its rear, was formed across the valley, at a retired point between 121 and 6, where its front could be generally swept by the artillery of the works on the Alhandra heights, and could also be closely flanked by a fire of musketry from some stone buildings, situated on the sides of the valley, which were converted into fortified posts.

Ultimately time being found, an additional post was established in rear of Mata Cruz, 125, which thoroughly connected the defence of Alhandra with that of the Serra de Serves, at its strongest point; and the front of that mountain from the bluff extremity above Portella to the pass of Bucellas, wherever deemed most accessible, was commenced to be scarped near its summit in imitation of Alhandra.*

On the left flank of the advanced defences, following up the course of the Zizandra (which in summer is an insignificant stream) to Torres Vedras, additional redoubts were thrown up to form a chain along the left bank of the river, and obstructions were created at points under their fire to the flow of the current, so that when the autumnal rains commenced, which happened the day that the advance of the army entered the lines, the river overflowed its banks, and in a short time more than half the valley became so complete a bog that no reward could induce any of the peasantry to attempt to pass over it; and that portion of the front which in summer had been the weakest, became, during the winter, in some degree secure from attack.

These two advanced flanks being thus strengthened, attention was naturally directed to a communication with the centre, and the invaders granting time, an interior line of road, for infantry and cavalry, was traced to connect Alhandra and Monte Agraça. All unnecessary access from the front was blocked up, and several bridges and paths leading to this ground

* These several works were superintended by Lieutenant Forster, having at different periods under his orders Lieutenants Trench, Piper, Tapp and Reid.

were destroyed, but no additional inclosed works were proposed. Indeed, from the left extremity of Alhandra, along the valley of Arruda to Mònte Agraça above Sobral, the hills being naturally bold and precipitous, and the communications from more than two-thirds of the salient features of the ground converging to a point, and passing over a narrow interior ridge, give this space a contracted second defence, which admits of limited numbers guarding its extended circumference; consequently the destruction of a few roads, blocking up the gorges of the ravines, and providing short lateral communications from the right and left to this interior line, were sufficient, in addition to the three or four redoubts previously established on the flanking points of the exterior ridge, to give great strength to this space, and ensure an uninterrupted communication from the Tagus to the great work on Monte Agraça.

On intelligence reaching Lisbon at the end of August, of the premature fall of Almeida, and the consequent retrograde movements of the protecting army, when the prospect of invasion seemed immediate, and the danger imminent, the fears of the public authorities induced ready attention to the urgent requisitions of the engineers for additional labour, and generated a momentary spirit of emulation to aid in the completion of the lines, now become the last bulwarks of the national independence. The conscription for labour was extended to a distance of more than fifty miles around; no excuse was admitted for withholding personal service—even women and boys took their share in the labour—and at one period, although the middle of harvest, the workmen on the lines were augmented to more than seven thousand. In consequence of such abundant labour, the months of August and September were most profitably occupied, besides erecting the new defences, in strengthening various points and works of the rear line, necessarily left imperfect when time appeared so very limited in the early summer; particularly at the position in front of Fort St. Julian's, covering the place of embarkation, at Mafra and the pass of Morugueira, and along the ravine to the left of that pass;* also on the position of Via Longa, and the low grounds bordering the Tagus.† At the former place, the eastern side of the valley in front of the quinta of the Marquis de Pombal was occupied by a detached work, No. 109, of strong profile, more than usually flanked, and the advanced heights were so shaped and scarped, as

* By Lieutenant Meinecke, King's German Legion, and Lieutenants Hulme and Reid.

† By Lieutenant Stanway.

to bring nearly all their reverse under fire of the artillery on the flanks of the defences. In aid of this measure, and to equalize the strength of the eastern front, the advanced defences of the main position beyond the little rivulet called Foz-de-Oeyras were joined by a line, No. 110, to the Tagus, so as to rest on Fort das Mais, by which additions the town of Oeyras was covered, and included within the exterior line of defence. On the left, the redoubts 106, 107, 108, were connected by a covered road or musketry trench to shelter infantry from a cannonade; but which being without a ditch in its front, and its parapet unreveted, admitted of a forward movement of the troops on any front, not exceeding the interval between two redoubts, or nearly 800 yards.*

As the army fell back on the lines by the most leisurely movements, time was also found to complete various services, which interfering with private establishments, or the public convenience, had been deferred to the latest moment, such as levelling obstructions to the fire of the works, felling the trees in their front, and forming substantial abattis with their stems and arms, breaking up roads, destroying bridges, preparing and charging mines, &c.; and on the

* By Captain Wedekind, King's German Legion.

7th of October, every preparation for defence was as complete as any longer delay could have rendered it.

The disposition of the irregular troops and the arrangements of the commissariat were also perfected during the leisurely retrograde movements of the army. The militia, ordenanza (national guards), and gunners, being assembled on the line of defence, and apportioned to the different works, were made to exercise the guns, and practise various defensive exercises; and depôts of provisions, tents, and stores were formed at points named from head-quarters.(3) The position and working of the signal stations were also perfected; and a party of seamen, supplied by the navy, now passed and received intelligence from one extremity of the line to the other in seven minutes, with undeviating accuracy; and as a further measure to ensure the communication of orders, arm telegraphs, constructed at Lisbon, were placed at each post in readiness to be used in the event of any disaster occurring to the masts or yards.

At this time also, the whole of the country which had been strengthened by works, was divided into six districts of nearly equal extent, and a regulating officer of engineers was appointed to each district for the purpose of explaining the nature and intention of the several fortified posts, to enable the general officers to take up their allotted ground in the most expeditious manner. (4) Mounted guides perfectly acquainted with all the localities were held in readiness at the most advanced points of each district to meet the columns, and assist the regulating officers in pointing out the several villages, bivouacs, &c. and afford such information respecting the various roads and communications as should prevent either confusion or mistake, should the enemy be pressing the columns.

The army, consisting of 22,000 British infantry, and 3,000 cavalry, with about a similar number of Portugueze infantry, entered the territory thus prepared for their reception and support, on the 8th of October, with the expectation of taking up the ground to dispute the principal passes of Mafra, Montachique, Bucellas, &c.; but their movements not being pressed by the invaders, (in consequence of the steady discipline preserved amongst the retiring troops, and the lesson they had given him at Busaco,) an embarrassment was felt about the points retrenched in advance, at Torres Vedras and Monte Agraça. To occupy them properly, would be to isolate and sacrifice a number of good troops without any object; whilst, to abandon, or leave them with inefficient garrisons to fall or capitulate, would be to furnish subject of triumph to the invaders, likely to produce the worst effects on the feelings of the troops and of the population. Lord Wellington, aware of the great strength which the heights of Alhandra, Calhandrix, &c. on the right flank of these posts had attained, and that the rains then pouring down with their accustomed autumnal violence must swell the Zizandra on their left flank and soon render it a formidable defensive obstacle, when there would remain from the sea to the Tagus only a space of about seven miles on the south of the valley of Runa, between Torres Vedras and Monte Agraça, without artificial defence, decided to halt at Sobral. The space last described presenting a most excellent field of battle for an army with an inferior cavalry, from having a strong and intersected front, and both flanks secure, he destined as the central point of his defensive manœuvres, placing the main body of his troops upon it, fixing his personal head-quarters at Pero Negro, immediately in its rear, and communicating with all parts of the line, from the telegraph on the elevated point of Monte Agraça forming its right flank.(5)

The redoubts and other defensive works being garrisoned with militia or ordenanzas, the troops composing the active army were thus distributed: General Hill's corps (two divisions) to guard the position of Alhandra; the light division, under General Craufurd, to occupy the front from the left of Alhandra, through Arruda, to the great work on Monte Agraça; the third division, under General Picton, to occupy Torres Vedras, and watch the line of the Zizandra; the fifth division, under General Leith, to take post on the reverse of the heights of Monte Agraça, with General Pack's independent Portugueze brigade, in the great redoubt on the summit of that mountain; and the first, fourth, and sixth divisions, under Generals Spencer, Cole and Campbell, to occupy Zibriera, Ribaldiera, Runa, &c., their left communicating with General Picton at Torres Vedras, and their right being in immediate contact with General Leith.

A corps of Spaniards under the Marquis de la Romana, about 6,000 infantry, which it had been arranged should cross the Tagus from Badajos at the same time that the army entered the lines, were to be placed on the intermediate post of Enxara dos Cavallieros.

The main body of the cavalry, which scarcely amounted to 3,000 men, were to be cantoned about the rear line, principally on the flanks, ready to act on the plains bordering the Tagus, or in the least broken tracts between the two lines, should a column of infantry have the temerity to penetrate into them by paths impracticable to cavalry and artillery.

The defence of Lisbon for some days, in the event of a total or partial discomfiture on the lines, was amply secured, without making any deduction from the effective force of the retiring army, by means of a powerful squadron collected in the Tagus, and a fine body of Marines sent from England, which, in addition to the civic corps, the militia, and the ordenanza of the district, and the ordinary garrison, directed by the British General Peacocke, formed an efficient as well as imposing force.

The army, which, during the retreat from Coimbra, had fallen back on one road, separated into two bodies at Pombal; General Picton's division marching from thence directly on Torres Vedras, and the remainder by the roads of Rio-mayor and Alemquer on Sobral, or Thomar and Santarem on Alhandra. On the 8th October the advance under General Hill reached the latter place. The previous night the autumnal rains had begun to fall in torrents, and continuing throughout the two following days, the newly formed communications became heavy and deep with mud; nevertheless, in consequence of the good arrangements previously made, the succeeding divisions marched directly on their allotted points of occupation, and separated at the fixed turnings, into brigades and battalions to their several villages and bivouacs, with as much celerity and order, as if re-entering their cantonments from a review.

On the 10th, the rear division, only distantly followed by the enemy, marched into Arruda, the preceding divisions took up ground on and beyond Monte Agraça, and a distribution of force was made for all the intermediate and rear defences.

During the succeeding night an unusually violent storm of wind and rain, thunder and lightning prevailed, which almost overwhelmed the troops in open bivouacs, and impeded the communication of orders; still, at daylight, on intelligence of the approach of the French, all were under arms in good order at their respective points of assembly, the garrison of the works complete and on the alert, the field artillery horsed or in position, and every other arrangement made to repel an attack. It was however late in the afternoon before the enemy began to act: Marshal Massena then with a strong body of cavalry dislodged the English post at Sobral, and ascended the height above the town, from whence he had a full view of the works opposed to him; and judging from their extent and formidable appearance that it was the intention seriously to dispute the ground, he withdrew his cavalry in the night, and Sobral was next morning re-occupied by strong British piquets.

The several divisions of the allies, as soon as posted on their ground, diligently employed themselves further to strengthen their respective fronts, particularly those forming the main body of the army between Monte Agraça and Runa, along which space no artificial defences had been previously established; the support of the advanced works by troops not having been contemplated in the original project for the lines. Indeed, from this cause even the great paved communication from Sobral to Zibriera, and the road from Sobral to Ribaldiera had not been blocked up by any work; so that in the position occupied by the allies the two armies might have come into contact without the invaders being under the necessity of forcing any defensive post.*

On the 13th, the French infantry having closed up, Marshal Massena directed a great effort against Sobral, which town not being

* To have placed the invaders under the necessity of storming, or otherwise reducing some work before they could bring forward their artillery, the height immediately in front of the town of Sobral de Monte Agraça should have been occupied.

within the line of defence was abandoned to him without a struggle. He immediately filled it with troops and closely supported them by other large bodies bivouacked in its immediate vicinity; these bodies communicating with the remainder of his army on the road of Alemquer. Having thus concentrated his whole force in readiness to act on the weakest point of the line, he pushed some strong patrols along the road of Zibriera and Ribaldiera to feel the allies, but which being quickly driven back, the advanced posts of the hostile armies arranged themselves almost in contact along the valley by Duas Portas towards Runa. The French cavalry piquets took post on the road between the town of Sobral and Monte Agraça with their videttes on the lower knolls of the mountain immediately under the great redoubt; and the remainder of the French army formed their bivouacs in the tract of country from Sobral to the Tagus, so as equally to threaten every part of the line from Zibriera to Alhandra, and their right being actually in contact with the weakest portion of it.

To strengthen the heights on the left of Monte Agraça consequently became an object of primary interest, and large working parties of the troops, frequently relieved, were unceasingly employed to throw up strong redoubts on the commanding points above Ribaldiera and Runa, 128, 129, and 130. The valley in rear of Gosandiera and Zibriera was blocked up by a well flanked abattis, field batteries of position were established on various flanking points of the same ground, and roads of communication formed to them, so that in a short time this open portion of the front quite changed its face, and appeared little less formidable than the other parts of the line.

Further, to parry this skilful disposition of the invading army, eight battalions from General Hill's corps were on the 14th formed in reserve on the second line, near the pass of Bucellas, in readiness to move at any moment to the support of Alhandra, or of the main body of the army by the roads of Zibriera and Sobral.

A redoubt, armed with 9-pounders, was also commenced on the ascent of Monte Agraça, on a lower level, and to the right of the main work, more effectually to enfilade and block up the great road from Sobral; and subsequently No. 149 was established above Matacaes, more completely to interdict the use of the road through the pass of Runa to the invaders, and the heights above Portella and Patameira were scarped, and strongly occupied by works 150 and 151. At the same time the defences behind the lower Zizandra were greatly augmented.

Every morning, two hours before day-break, the troops stood to their arms at the point of assembly of their several cantonments, as did also the garrisons of the works; Lord Wellington, in person, being in the fort on Monte Agraça, in readiness to direct any general movement, according to the exigencies of the moment. The army thus remained under arms till a communication from every portion of the line, and ocular demonstration, had assured their commander, that no change had taken place in the disposition of the hostile troops, nor any preparation been made for immediate attack; the several divisions and brigades were then ordered to resume their daily labours of strengthening their respective fronts, making lateral communications, improving the roads, sheltering and securing their outposts, &c. The weather was generally wet, and the duty irksome—still all supported it with cheerfulness, in the full confidence of annihilating their opponent, whenever the threatened attack should take place; but after a week had elapsed, expectation would no longer support itself, and the hope of an immediate and brilliant triumph subsided.

Marshal Massena made in person a very

close reconnoissance of the right of the lines, and on the 16th, having remained an unusual time with a numerous staff examining the entry of the valley of Calhandrix, a shot was fired at the party from No. 120, which striking a wall whereon the Marshal was resting his telescope, he acknowledged the warning by taking off his hat, and moving on.* This reconnoissance served to convince the French commander of the inadequacy of his means to attack an army so posted and supported, he therefore turned all his views to subsist his forces till he could be reinforced; and after remaining in his original bivouacs till he had exhausted the country, and his troops were becoming sickly, he retired on the night of the 14th November towards Santarem, and was next day closely followed by Lord Wellington.

Marshal Massena took up a defensive line behind the Rio Major, entrenching a corps at Santarem, and the allies went into cantonments at Cartaxo (head-quarters), Alcoentre, Azam-

* There was no wish to injure Marshal Massena, but merely to make him retire, or a dozen guns might as readily have been discharged at him as one. Napoleon, who always spoke and reasoned well on military subjects, has left recorded, in Count Las Casas' Journal, an excellent observation on the folly of firing a single piece of ordnance at an individual where injury is meditated.

buja, Alemquer, Villa Franca, &c. one division being left at Torres Vedras, and the whole kept in readiness to fall back whenever the French should be greatly reinforced; under which expectation every exertion was ordered to be made to keep up and improve the works of the lines.

In aid of a protracted defence of the peninsula of Lisbon, Abrantes had been enclosed with works, and the fortifications of Peniche had been repaired and augmented. The good effect of these measures now became apparent, as frequent sorties from Peniche kept the cantonments of the invaders in a state of watchfulness and alarm; whilst Abrantes, blocked to the French, and kept open to the allies the best communication across the Tagus.

Peniche was in all respects a fortress; but there being no possibility of transporting heavy artillery across the Serra de Estrella, for the attack of Abrantes, its defences were limited to a resistance against a coup-de-main, or an attack with twelve-pounders.*

The garrison of Abrantes was composed altogether of troops in the service of Portugal,

* The armament of the place was limited to the calibre of a 12-pounder, to prevent the invaders forming a battering train in the event of their capturing it.

commanded by a Portuguese governor. The only British in the place were the engineers, the senior of whom, Captain Patton, (the officer who had constructed the defences,) being a man of peculiar gallantry and firmness, was, by order of Lord Wellington, made one of a council of defence, and any proposition for surrender was forbidden to be tendered or received without his name being signed in approval of the measure.

Marshal Massena early saw the importance of Abrantes, to secure a communication with and enable him to draw supplies from the Alemtejo; and, previously to retiring from before the lines, caused the works to be closely reconnoitered, when they were deemed too strong to be attempted by a coup-de-main.

To prevent the invaders communicating with the Alemtejo by any other point, the right corps of the allies, under Marshal Beresford, had, on the change of position of the hostile armies, been passed over the Tagus in boats, and cantoned at Barcos, Chamusca, &c.: floating bridges were now established on all the small rivers in its rear to the ferry opposite Alhandra, to ensure its re-occupation of that point, should it become necessary.

In the beginning of December, some movements of the French troops in the south of

Spain leading to the belief of a diversion being intended in the Alemtejo, in aid of renewed operation against the lines, the promontory of Almada, on the left of the Tagus, opposite to Lisbon, which commands the navigation of the river, and from whence shells will range over a great portion of the city,* was retrenched under the superintendence of Captain Goldfinch.

The left of the position rested on the broad basin of the Tagus, on the heights immediately above Mutella; its centre was on Monte de Caparica, Lugar de Monte, and its right on the rocky cliff called the Altos da Raposeira, rising above the sea, the whole extent of its front being about 8000 yards. A chain of redoubts, 17 in number, flanking each other, and having fleches in their front, more completely to see into the ravines, was established on the most prominent knolls of this line, their defence being united with, and supported by, several country-houses in their rear, which, being built of stone, with stone enclosures, might at any moment be rendered formidable posts. A sunken road, which extended nearly throughout the position, in rear of the redoubts, formed a

* The Tagus, opposite the Castle of Almada, is only 2,200 yards in width.

secure communication between them, and was ingeniously made by the executive officer to add to their defence, by cutting a banquette, and dressing off the slope in its front so as to form it into a regular covered way, with places of arms at points which gave the best flanks and could best be supported from the stone buildings.*

The dilapidated castle of Almada was repaired and armed for defence, so as to form a species of interior citadel, which should preserve the communication with Lisbon till the latest moment; and as a means of ready communication between the fleet and the several parts of the position, roads were carried up various parts of the cliff, forming its gorge.

It being proposed to entrust the defence of this position to the seamen and marines of the fleet, with the militia and civic corps of Lisbon, the redoubts were made of unusual magnitude, many being capable of containing 4, 5, or 600 men, and from 6 to 10 pieces of artillery; the calculated garrisons for the whole when com-

* After a certain portion of this road had been formed, the completion of the remainder was suspended, in consequence of the inconvenience it occasioned to the occupiers of private dwellings, and the knowledge that the road could, by due attention, be finished whenever required in less time than an invader could collect a force, and march through the Alemtejo.

pleted being 7,500 men and 86 pieces of ordnance. Any attack of Almada at this time could only have been a secondary operation; for, even if successful, the Tagus would still have interposed an impassable obstacle between the victors and Lisbon, and their retention of the promontory must have been altogether contingent on success in front. Therefore any mode of occupation of Almada, which should have prejudiced the defence of the lines, could scarcely have been justified; but it was an object of the greatest value thus, by means of strong works and a force which could not otherwise have been rendered serviceable, to have done away the possibility of a small corps annoying the fleet, creating alarm and confusion in the capital, and perhaps spreading a panic throughout the country in rear of the army, at the moment of the lines being attacked.

During the winter the posts of the two armies remained as first arranged on either side of the Rio-Major, the advance of the French being retrenched at Santarem, and that of the allies occupying the village of Val; the hostile sentinels being only separated by the bridge at the south western extremity of the long causeway across the marsh between the two places. Each stood unremittingly on the alert, the allies trusting to a mine, which they kept ready for explosion under the principal arch of the bridge, to prevent a sudden rush; and the French to the artillery of a redoubt, which they had constructed on a height enfilading the whole length of the communication. On the left flank the armies were not in such immediate contact, the allies being entrenched at Alcoentre with a piquet of observation in the town of Rio-major, and the principal force of the French being at Alcanhede; nevertheless the same vigilance was maintained as on the right. On the left of the Tagus, besides lining the bank of the river with piquets of observation, batteries were thrown up to command the mouth of the Zezere, where the French had collected many boats, and the ruined castle of Tancos was converted into a military post.

During this time unremitting care and attention was also paid to strengthen the several defences of the lines, add to the scarps, and perfect the lateral communications; for which latter object a paved road communicating with the rear by Pero Negro, was ordered to be formed along the rear of the heights last retrenched on the left of Monte Agraça, and a communication for carriages was made from the left of Alhandra across the valley of Calhandrix by St. Romeo, and in rear of the pass of Matos, to Monte Agraça; and subsequently similarly ready and short communications were perfected throughout the whole tract of fortified country. As the spring advanced additional works, mounted with 56 pieces of ordnance, were completed behind the Zizandra, No. 131 to 144, and the left bank of that river was scarped to compensate the fall of the waters and preserve the equilibrium of defence.

The bridges on the great road from the rear of the cantonments of the army to the front of the lines were mined for destruction, those on the lateral communications destroyed, and all obstructions to the fire of gun-boats on the road or ground bordering the Tagus, were levelled.

It is almost unnecessary to add, that no renewed effort against the lines was made to put the value of these labours to the test. The invaders, after remaining in their cantonments till the commencement of March, retired out of the country, closely pursued and harassed by the allies; offering the first and only instance of a military enterprise planned and matured by Napoleon, whilst in the plenitude of his power, being defeated by the steady perseverance and superior foresight of an opponent. It is not, perhaps, too much to add, that this failure before Lisbon gave a fatal blow to the general belief of French invincibility, and taught oppressed Europe to resist and become free.

CHAPTER II.

GENERAL OBSERVATIONS ON THE LINES COVERING LISBON.

From the foregoing description it will be seen that the lines covering Lisbon consisted of two distinct ranges of hills, or rather tracts of country, extending from the sea to the Tagus, modelled into strong fields of defensive action and defensive manœuvres; each line in some degree aiding the other, but their occupation and defence being perfectly distinct and independent.

On a comparison of the two lines, it must be admitted that, looking to operations during summer, the rear line appears to have been judiciously selected for the arena of defence, as it contains the greatest portion and most equal distribution of strength of front. Thus the greater part of the ravine from Ribamar to Mafra is very strong, whereas no portion of the banks of the Zizandra below Torres Vedras is otherwise than tame. In like manner the passes of Montachique and Bucellas are of the strongest nature of mountain pass, whilst the corresponding inlets of Zibriera and Monte Agraça derived their strength chiefly from works. The rear defences have also the advantage over the advanced line of covering four or five miles less ground; the former, following the principal features of defence, measuring 24 miles, and the latter 29 miles. The distance in a direct line between their flanks being 22 and 25 miles respectively. Further, under the belief that the invaders would approach in sufficient force to act in two bodies, and the impression then general throughout Europe, that the French could not fail of success, it was an advantage of the rear line not to be despised, that its strongest flank was nearest the point of retreat and embarkation, and consequently that least likely to be forced.

In any extremity arising from an overwhelming pursuit, and a harassed retrograde march, the rear defences would therefore in all probability have formed the field of proffered combat; but, under the favorable circumstances of the young Portugueze troops having proved themselves trust-worthy, a triumphant retreat, and an advanced season, with an enemy acting only on one point, to have left the advanced works to their garrisons, and to have abandoned to the invaders 150 additional square miles of country contained in the space between the two lines, would have been a sacrifice of character, feeling, and confidence, far beyond what any increase of physical strength could have compensated; and here, as ought to be in every case depending on judgment, previous arrangement was modified, and made to give way to circumstances.

From the distribution of the troops in the lines it appears that Lord Wellington, under the expectation of fighting a battle which should decide the fate of a kingdom, spread an army not amounting to 50,000 men along a front of 29 miles. This extended arrangement is so contrary to the spirit of modern warfare,* that to prevent any erroneous conclusions being drawn from it, it is deemed necessary to mention that the allotment of the force for the several portions of the line was calculated on a peculiarity of the features of the country, as well as on the extraordinary degree of strength which had been given to the flanks, rendering them rather fortresses of support than points to guard. The peculiarity alluded to is the projection of Monte Junto, which stretches out fifteen miles in front of the centre of the lines, and is of so rugged and precipitous a formation, as to preclude the march of an army with artillery over its sum-

* It is remarkable, that the most striking example of concentration also during the late wars should have been afforded by this same commander, who, at Waterloo, placed and manœuvred 60,000 men on a front little exceeding a mile and a half.

mit; nor can the ridge of Barregudo, which nearly connects Monte Junto with the position, be crossed with artillery without a publicity and delay which would have deprived the movement of every advantage; and the ridge can only be avoided by passing along the road of Runa, which was included within the line of defence. These serras consequently divide the attack and defence of the front line into two portions, giving the assailants a very long and tedious march to move a corps from opposite Alhandra to the line of the Zizandra below Torres Vedras; whereas, from the position of the main body of the army between Torres Vedras and Monte Agraça, a very short march would enable the defenders to succour either the right or left, and compensate inferiority of numbers by superiority of movement.

It may also be observed, in further justification of this unusual extension, that the celerity and accuracy with which, by means of the signal stations, orders could be sent and intelligence received from the most distant points of the lines, obliterated distance with respect to communication and ensured a well timed combination of movement amongst the whole body of the defenders, enabling them to derive every advantage from partial success and protecting them from overwhelming disaster in the event of partial discomfiture.

As a general character of the lines, formed from unprejudiced consideration of their merits and defects, it may be stated that they derived their strength and value primarily from their peninsular situation on the sea, which precluded the possibility of an enemy manœuvring on, or turning their flanks, and assured their rear being constantly open for the defenders to receive supplies and reinforcements; secondly, from the unusual degree of natural strength of the ranges of hills and ravines forming their front; and lastly from the judgment with which the engineer connected the several strong features of the country into an equally defensive line. Art and labour were judiciously exerted to improve natural advantages, to strengthen and cover the weak points, to diminish the length of accessible front, to block up the approaches, to facilitate the movements of troops within, and to cramp and confine the movements of those without; in short, to give such powers of defence and communication to every portion of the front that the army might remain concentrated in a body, keeping only detached corps of observation on its right and left, which, from the natural and artificial strength of their positions, might repel a weak or sustain a serious attack till succoured; and that at no point should a corps engage, but under the favourable circumstances of a strong front, secure flanks, facility of movement, and an open, but inattackable rear.

The redoubts, generally speaking, were merely securities for artillery in those situations where a fire of that nature was demanded by some specific object, such as to interdict the free use of a road, delay the repair of a bridge, or sweep along the entry of a pass; and in no instance were the guns considered as defensive weapons of the works in which they were placed, except at the position on the height of Calhandrix, where three redoubts in line were made to cross their fire with each other, and mutually support a fourth redoubt in advance. All the other redoubts were perfectly independent of each other, and were made of a strength of profile to resist an assault, and placed on points where artillery could with great difficulty be brought to cannonade them. Their number was justified by the peculiarity of the contest, which placed, on the same position with a good army, half the same amount of militia, ill-organized peasantry and gunners who, though totally unfit to act in the field, still being possessed of innate courage, were equal to defend a redoubt and work its artillery. Throughout the whole front there was not a continuity of artificial line necessitating a single efficient brigade to be kept out of column, and the works may be regarded as so much additional strength given to the army, without subtracting a man from its effective force. Indeed the artificial defences of the lines altogether present a most favourable example of the just application of the engineer's art in furtherance of, but invariably subservient to tactics, creating pivots and supports, but never a tie or restraint on field-movements.

In appreciating the defensive power of the various portions of the lines against the efforts of an invader only moderately superior to the defenders, this consideration of the defensive army being a compact and manœuvring body totally independent of the works should have great weight; as, in consequence, it would not have sufficed for the ultimate triumph of the assailants that a column should manœuvre successfully so as to fall on some weakly guarded point, before the defenders could be reinforced. By such a movement the assaulting force would only have lent a flank and offered a most advantageous opportunity for the attack of an army, ready to engage with it; or even should the assailants by a rapid and powerful effort have broken through any point of the line, it would have served merely to place them between an efficient army and a city which, though not fortified, was assuredly far beyond a coup-de-main.*

Therefore notwithstanding their many natural and professional merits, it must be acknowledged that the troops were to the lines as life and health to the body, giving them strength and efficiency in exact proportion to their own; and that a successful defence of the lines hinged altogether on the unremitting vigilance, able disposition, and rapid movement of the defenders. One single error of judgment, or one single miscalculation of time or distance might have rendered the whole line of works useless; for field-redoubts left to their own garrisons, even when thickly studded, can only be expected to impede, turn or disorganize a column of march with its artillery, but never to oppose an impenetrable barrier to the advance of a powerful and determined army.

* In order that an army covering a capital should preserve due latitude of manœuvring, it is indispensable that the city should be rendered capable of several days resistance when left to its own powers. A variety of instances might be adduced in proof of this statement: but two very recent and well-known examples will suffice:—In 1813 Napoleon, by his foresight and activity in throwing up works on the banks of the Elbe, preserved Dresden during one of his manœuvres, and in 1814 lost Paris during a similar manœuvre from having too tardily and insufficiently fortified it.

CHAPTER III.

OBSERVATIONS ON LINES AND RETRENCHED POSITIONS GENERALLY.*

Ceux qui proscrivent les lignes et tous les secours que l'art de l'ingenieur peut donner se privent gratuitement d'une force et d'un moyen auxiliaires jamais nuisibles, presque toujours utiles et souvent indispensables.

UNTIL recent experience, it was fast becoming an axiom, that an army receiving battle in position must be beaten, and that no skill in occupying and strengthening, nor firmness in disputing and maintaining ground, could balance the advantage of free and concentrated movement, and the moral confidence arising from being the assailant. The recorded sentiments and feelings of many celebrated commanders and tacticians are in unison with this opinion; and with the solitary exception of the battle of Fontenoy, the page of history uniformly supports it, from the actions of Blenheim and Ramilies,

* This chapter was originally composed as the vehicle for a series of notes illustrative of the principles of field fortification, and of the art of fortifying generally, but which are too bulky to insert in this pamphlet.

through the operations of Frederick and Napoleon, to the campaigns in Egypt and the Peninsula. There the reverse was for the first time exemplified in a succession of brilliant triumphs on the defensive fields of Alexandria, Corunna, Talavera, Albuera, Fuentes de Honor, the Pyrenees; and in front of Lisbon, the exploded opinion, after the interval of a century, was revived and happily exemplified, of lines being able to check and paralyse the efforts of a powerful invader.

Whether these successes should be ascribed to the ability with which the several positions were occupied or retrenched, to the superiority of the troops, or to the *impassible* nature of Englishmen as our opponents state; or whether there be advantages to be derived from defensive combat not understood by other armies, it is not deemed necessary to inquire. But as from the inadequate force with which we usually carry on continental operations, defensive warfare sustained in defensive positions must continue to be resorted to, some general observations on the subject of retrenching ground and positions have been thrown together with the view of leading the young officer to form a correct judgment as to the value and proper application of field-defences—that he may neither despise them as altogether useless to an army, nor trust to them as never-failing sources of strength.

On the first of these points it must be recollected that, although during the early part of the last war field-works fell into discredit, and almost into disuse, such aids were previouly very highly estimated by those best able to judge of their utility. Frederick II., Marshal Saxe, Count Daun, and all the best generals of the last century, frequently and successfully availed themselves of redoubts and retrenchments to strengthen their positions or support their movements; and it is a well-established historical fact, that a few earthern redoubts at Pultawa marred the fortune of Charles XII. and fixed the wavering destinies of the great Muscovite empire.

It is, however, unnecessary to revert to past history to show the value of field-works, as in the recent battle of Borodino, a few simple redans hastily thrown up to cover the left flank of the Russian position paralysed for hours two French corps d'armée, and had nearly proved equally fatal to the fortunes of Napoleon as the redoubts at Pultawa to those of his prototype Charles. Indeed the attack of Dresden, which failed in consequence of the assailants being opposed by a slight field-retrenchment, and many other events of the recent campaigns, leave no doubt that field-works judiciously disposed may still be rendered valuable auxiliaries, even to the most numerous and most active armies.

To effect this, and apportion works justly to cover a country, or strengthen a proposed field of battle, is the most difficult application of the engineer's art, being subject to no fixed rule, but merely founded on general principles, requiring to be modified on each occasion from an innumerable variety of circumstances, both physical and moral.

A just idea of these principles can only be acquired through a knowledge of tactics, and of the powers of troops under different orders of formation and movement; which, well understood, can scarcely fail to produce a feeling that works ought in every situation to be accessaries and aids to the manœuvres of troops, and never principals of any defensive field-system.

Posting troops to fight a general action, or strengthening the front of an army when so posted, are details founded on the foregoing principles, which for the same reasons scarcely admit of theoretic elucidation, and the knowledge of them can only be fully attained by long service with an active corps.

Considerable insight into such details may,

however, be gained by studying the principles on which various fields of defensive combat have been occupied by skilful commanders.

In these it will be seen that a rocky height, a knoll, a wood, a village, and even a single house, have frequently formed the prominent flank or defensive posts; and instances might be adduced where each of the above obstacles have mainly contributed to the repulse of the assailants; and on the contrary, where such posts, injudiciously occupied or ill-supported, have led to discomfiture or the loss of entire divisions of the defensive force.

These extremes are found in the battles of Blenheim in 1704, and of Ligny, in 1815.

In the former action, the village of Blenheim, on the left flank of the defensive army, being well retrenched and occupied with twenty-four battalions and twelve squadrons, proved an insurmountable obstacle to the Duke of Marlborough's efforts in the early part of the action; but that commander skilfully transferring his attack to a point near the centre of the defensive line, which was beyond molestation from the troops in Blenheim, they, from principals in the action, became merely spectators of the defeat of their friends when they had no alternative but to surrender prisoners. At the battle of Ligny, on the contrary, the town and villages in front of the Prussian line on the heights of Sombref were so strongly occupied with men, and so closely supported each other, that Napoleon did not dare to leave them in his rear or on his flanks, but wasted his time and exhausted his strength during many hours in an attack of advanced posts, till too late to force the Prussian line, which retired without loss as soon as it became dark.

But to leave these higher points, as also the best formation of troops, the situations of the artillery, and the dispositions of the reserve, which are usually settled in all their details by the general in chief, and confining ourselves to the consideration of the best means of strengthening troops already posted, we may adduce the battle of Waterloo as a happy exemplification of natural defences being turned to profit.

In that action the line being formed along the crest of a range of easy heights, the country-house of Goumont was very strongly and the farm buildings of La Haye Sainte moderately occupied as posts in advance of the line; the former being in front of the right flank, at the distance of four hundred yards, and the latter nearly in front of the centre, at the distance of three hundred yards, the interval between them being thirteen hundred yards.

Napoleon did not think it prudent to pass

through this space, or leave two such posts in rear of his attacking columns, and as a preliminary measure to advancing against the line, made a great effort to possess himself of Goumont.

The column for the attack was of a magnitude, and advanced with an intrepidity which seemed to command success, as did a second and third, supported by a powerful fire of artillery; but the battalions of Guards which occupied the building, being experienced as well as brave troops, had most judiciously loop-holed the garden walls to the front, and otherwise so opened their fire, that they maintained the post, and covered the right flank of the position throughout the day.

The Germans in La Haye Sainte behaved with similar firmness, and long disputed the passage of the chaussée; but their communications being cut off,* and their numbers too few to be formidable to the rear or flank of an advancing column, Napoleon concentrated on their left a most powerful body of troops, which advanced to attack the line with apparently

* Their communications and the post itself were ultimately lost from neglect of the simple precaution of blocking up the entrance gate at the side, and forming an opening through the rear enclosure wall; which would have admitted of the ammunition of the defenders being renewed, and their casualties replaced.

matchless force; but a slight bank and hedge enabled a very inferior force to check their progress till troops came up from the second line and utterly routed them.

It is evident that on the field of Waterloo, or on any other field of defensive combat, with time, artificial defences might have been prepared on or near the sites of the buildings or hedges occupied by the troops in advance of the main line, which would have afforded an

* In order to prevent any misconception from the above observations, it is necessary to state that no artificial cover or retrenchments of any nature aided the firmness of the troops, and that the battle of Waterloo was fought on ground untouched by the spade.

The present appearance of the field, however, seems to contradict this fact, and will, after a few years, afford plausible arguments for historic doubts on the subject. The excavations recently made along the front of the position, to obtain soil to raise the artificial mountain on which the Belgic Lion now peers over the field, have the precise trace and appearance of a well-flanked retrenchment; and further, the artificial mountain itself forms a strong and commanding feature, which, if viewed as part of the position, takes away nearly all the merit of its defence.

Indeed it is truly to be regretted that the good citizens of Brussels should, in the gratification of civic vanity, have had the bad taste to destroy a lasting and indisputable memorial of the valor and firmness of their countrymen and their allies, merely to substitute a perishable trophy of their own loyalty, which will in all probability be thrown down on the first ephemeral success of a French army.

equal or better defence; and thus we discover at once the position in which works would positively have aided an army.

Other battles are equally illustrative of the use of strengthening the most prominent or marked features of defensive ground, either with the view of covering a weak front by an advanced or flanking fire, or preventing an assailant from establishing his artillery on points favourable for cannonading the defensive line previously to using his bayonet; and even where such marked features of the ground do not exist, their place may readily be supplied artificially by the erection of flanked works, or two or more, or a system of redoubts flanking each other, in such situations and force as experience will soon teach an officer to be necessary.

There is, however, a very serious obstacle to the employment of the art of retrenching positions, which is, that after an army has taken up its ground and a battle becomes inevitable, there is seldom time to throw up works of sufficient strength to be depended upon; and it is scarcely possible, in any moderately open country, to select a position to be fortified in advance for the protection of a frontier or a capital which an enemy will not find roads to turn and render useless. Thus, in allusion to the battle of Waterloo, had the ground been strongly retrenched during the spring, Napoleon would naturally have avoided it by marching on Brussels by the road of Hal, and therefore such preparatory labours seem only advisable in peninsular situations, or to block up the entry, or dispute the sortie of a mountain-pass, occupy the interval between two fortresses, or for some other specific and very limited object.*

Even in such favourable situations, attention should be directed rather to the improvement of natural obstacles, than to the erection of artificial lines of defence; and where works cannot be dispensed with, they should, as far as practicable, be inclosed, independent, and capable of defending themselves. Nothing can be more vicious than to cover an extensive tract of country with a regular system of bastions and redans, as recommended in most treatises on field-fortification. Such long systematic lines of defensive works, besides the great expense, labour and publicity attending

* The Duke of Wellington, in his defensive campaigns, felt this so strongly, that on some occasions (near Campomair, in 1811, for instance) where he strengthened open ground with the intention of giving battle, he caused the parties to labour during the obscurity of night only, and the excavation to be covered at break of day with boughs, so as not to be recognized as works by the enemy from the neighbouring heights.

their formation, have the serious defect of being of no strength, unless equally guarded throughout; and further, when attacked, the defenders have, in consequence of their flanked trace, to man an alignment of nearly double the length of the front to be defended, and are utterly incapacitated from making any instantaneous or powerful forward movement; they therefore necessitate the worst possible disposition of troops for offence or defence, and must be regarded as inadmissible under the present system of tactics. Indeed, such long defensive lines, even when most in repute at the end of the seventeenth and commencement of the eighteenth century, were invariably forced as often as attacked, and it is difficult to conceive on what foundation their popularity so long sustained itself.

Field-defences, however, are not to be indiscriminately condemned or rejected, because they are continuous or systematic. In order to strengthen the front of an army with judgment, it is necessary to consider every feature and every portion of the ground separately, and arrange such mode of occupation as shall best combine its particular defence with the general defence of the position. Thus, in parts unfavourable for manœuvring, it may be advisable to form a continued line of considerable extent covered with every nature of obstacle, and having none but the most confined outlets, on the principle that a range of difficult heights would be scarped, or low ground inundated, to lessen the number of men on those points, and leave a superabundance of force for other points favourable for offensive movements. Again, since the employment of artillery in masses has been introduced, and that an irresistible fire, sometimes of hours duration, now invariably precedes the advance of the columns of attack, it will frequently prove a good measure, in situations where natural cover cannot be formed from a cannonade to create it artificially between all the prominent defensive posts.* Thus each furlong of ground being duly considered, and the nature of defence best adapted to the locality being formed, the whole front of an army may occasionally be covered with lines of works, which, while they augment its defensive powers, leave its movements perfectly free.

Continuous lines, of the short extent of a mile or two, may frequently be resorted to with

* This might be effected by means of a sunken trench, like a parallel at a siege, made to connect a whole chain of redoubts. Such an expedient would cover infantry from the fire of guns without impeding their forward movement in line, and openings might be left for the advance of the cavalry and artillery, or they might act in masses on the flanks.

advantage, in situations where the flanks can be naturally or artificially secured, as on a river or a fortress.

Such lines, in communication with a fortified town, when composed of fronts of fortification or other flanked trace, and made of a profile not to be assaulted, are well suited to facilitate the defensive manœuvres of an inferior army, and also to augment the defensive powers of the fortress itself, by occupying important tracts of ground which could not be included within the permanent works. In such cases they are usually denominated retrenched camps, as at Setuval, Bayonne, Antwerp, &c. under which character they form a medium of defence between field-works and permanent fortifications, which can be resorted to on any pressing emergency arising from defeat, and may be generally recommended by an officer without hesitation; for if it be not convenient to man them fully, their evacuation after a show of resistance neither compromises the retreat of the defenders, nor detracts from the original strength of the fortress.

Experience affords many proofs of positions of two or three miles length of front, which could not be turned, when retrenched on a field profile, being capable of an excellent defence; and our own annals furnish a remarkable instance, in the attack by the Duke of Marlborough, of a small córps hastily and imperfectly retrenched at Donawert, in June, 1704, when an incomplete victory cost the Duke 8 general officers, 1,500 men killed, and 4,000 wounded,* being a greater loss than he experienced in the July following, in forcing Marshal Villeroy's extensive lines of Tirlemont, defended by 70,000 men: and on this point it should be recollected, that the most sanguinary and least complete victory of the same celebrated commander was over an army in a retrenched position of short front at Malplaquet.

It is apparent, however, that isolated and unsupported field-positions of this nature, retrenched on a field-profile, besides being liable to be turned, and the defenders shut up as in a trap and made prisoners, partake of all the defects of longer continued lines in proportion to their extent, and are in the same proportion objectionable. They are, consequently, inadmissible whilst hostilities are carried on with the numerous and powerful armies of the present day, and would scarcely have demanded an observation had not the most prominent example of a retrenched field-position ever formed in England been of such nature.

* See Life of Marlborough, by Archdeacon Coxe, vol. i., p. 259.

None of the objections to continuous lines, however, apply to retrenchments formed of enclosed and isolated works, each capable of a good resistance, as the intervals between them do not require a line of supporting troops, and after furnishing garrisons for the works, the army may remain in masses sheltered from cannonade by some irregularity of the ground near the summit of the heights; or if such be not found, on their reverse, immediately below the crest, ready to move in compact and formidable bodies on any menaced point, or form into line or manœuvre on the posts taken up, so as best to parry the efforts of the assailants; a good specimen of which nature of position may be studied in the defences of Almada.

It seems to be an indispensable condition of such field-works in aid of an army, whether prepared at leisure or during active operations, that they be of a profile and capability of defence to resist an assault, that they be securely closed in the rear, placed sufficiently near to and so disposed as to flank each other, and armed with sufficient artillery to prevent heavy columns passing between them without being thrown into disorder from severe loss; or else made of a size to contain a force likely to prove formidable to the rear of a column which should venture to pass them. In this case, indeed in all cases, the outlets from, and intervals between works, should give every freedom for the movement of troops compatible with security from assault or being passed.

On this point it may be as well to observe, that detached enclosed works, in front of an inferior army acting on the defensive, ought to be regarded as vital points performing certain functions of themselves, and their garrisons be considered as integral parts of the works, destined to share their fate—to triumph or fall with their post, and not as portions of the army to be protected and withdrawn. Under this view the defensive corps being left unshackled in their movements, and their part being confined to the discomfiture of the enemy, they will be prepared to seize the favourable moment, and advance to the attack when the redoubts shall be most warmly engaged, or their fire have thrown the assailants into confusion; so that to derive full benefit from works, as much judgment is required in posting and manœuvring the force to be strengthened, as in placing the works themselves.

This leads to a consideration of the just proportion between the garrisons of detached works and the army they cover, and also of the length of front along which works may be allowed to extend for given numbers of men.

On the first point it may be observed, that the better the troops composing the defensive army, the fewer should be the works, for it can seldom be advisable to confine any considerable body of a manœuvring and steady force in an enclosed work, unless it be the key or main support of a position;* but when an army is composed in great part of ill-disciplined and unsteady troops artificial defences can scarcely be too numerous.

The extent of front which works may cover need in strictness only be limited by the power the army possesses of succouring, in sufficient time, any and every work that may be pressed, so that a ready or difficult communication will frequently decide the eligibility of occupying a distant point; but as strength is invariably gained by concentration, no ground should be occupied that is not intimately connected with the main object of defence, even if invitingly convenient. On this head no better rule can be followed than to inquire, previously to occupying any point, whether it be essential to the support or safety of the main body of the army; and on each occasion, an officer must exercise his judgment, to modify and turn local circumstances to advantage on the unchange-

* Such, for instance, as the occupation of Goumont by the Guards at Waterloo.

able basis of science. It cannot however be too strongly borne in mind by those planning defensive expedients, that troops are the principals, works the accessaries of defence, that the latter must invariably be dependent on and limited by the former, and consequently that every point superfluously retrenched is an unnecessary source of distraction and division of force. Field-works can never without hazard be left to their own garrisons; and reverting to the lines of Torres Vedras, which would seem to warrant the creation of an unlimited number of defences, it may be confidently predicted that any commander not possessing the utmost promptitude, decision and skill in manœuvring troops, who, trusting to that example, shall attempt to defend against a superior, or even equal force, a tract of four-and-twenty miles of country as a fortified position, will infallibly be beaten; and that an engineer who should, on any ordinary occasion, copy the extended system of isolated redoubts and retrenchments practised in front of Lisbon, would, instead of adding to the strength, altogether cripple an army.

But whenever, by the foresight and skill of the general and the exertion of the engineer, the arrangements of the troops and works shall be in happy unison, and a defensive army well posted shall have its front covered with works constructed on just principles, its force will be incalculably augmented, and its defeat rendered almost impracticable. Even a few works, thus judiciously disposed on the principal features of the ground, or to sweep the approaches, could not fail to add materially to the powers of movement and resistance of a defensive force;* as will frequently the most trifling efforts of labour, such as loop-holing buildings, barricading streets, blocking up or opening communications, destroying bridges or roads, or the fords of a river, felling abattis, forming emplacements for field-guns, or the slightest cover from cannonade; and an active and zealous engineer will generally find opportunity on the eve of a battle to strengthen, by some of these various labours, the fronts and flanks of a defensive force.

In making this statement it is not forgotten, that since the improved organization of armies has given them an increased facility of movement, and a consequent celerity and boldness of enterprise, placing legs almost on an equality with

* Napoleon was so highly impressed with the value of these preliminary labours, even where armies are nearly balanced in strength, that on the morning of the battle of Austerlitz he went at the break of day to the retrenchment of Santon, and remained there for a considerable time on foot, encouraging and urging on the exertions of the working party.

arms in war, time is rarely allowed to a defensive force for perfecting defensive expedients; but this consideration so far from being deemed to excuse the attempt, should only stimulate an engineer to increased exertion. The country naturally expects some return for the liberal arrangements recently made to improve the engineer's service, and increase the engineer's means, and every officer is interested to show that the sappers and their field-equipment, which now form an integral part of each division of an army, are available auxiliaries to its force. The most simple exercise of his art will occasionally prove their paramount utility; and as it not unfrequently occurs, even after hostile armies come into view, that days pass in reconnoitering or preparation for attack, who can say on such occassions to what extent activity and intelligence may not gain artificial strength for a field of defensive action, and consequent character and reputation for an officer?

CHAPTER IV.

MEMORANDA RELATING TO VARIOUS DETAILS OF FIELD-WORKS AS THROWN UP ON THESE LINES.

(Plates 1, 2, 3, 4, and 5.)

Les principes des fortifications de campagne ont besoin d'être perfectionnés : cette partie de l'art de la guerre est susceptible de faire de grands progrès.

Les fortifications de campagne sont toujours utiles—jamais nuisibles, lorsqu'elles sont bien entendues.—*Conversationes de Napoleon, par Montholon.*

Workmen.—The manual labour of the lines was performed by the peasantry of the country and two regiments of militia. The former were obtained by conscription and were relieved weekly; the latter worked as a permanent duty. The peasantry were paid six vintems per day as labourers, and twelve vintems per day as mechanics, and the militia at one third those rates.* Subsequently as the work increased and lengthened almost into a permanent occupation for the peasantry, their rate of wages was augmented to ten vintems per diem for labourers, and sixteen for artificers, the militia continuing to be paid at the original rate. In August, 1810,

* A vintem is 5·4 farthings.

when more than 2,500 men were working in a body at Alhandra, and the ordinary supply of the town would not furnish sufficient provisions for such augmented numbers, the officers of engineers took upon themselves to make requisitions on the neighbouring districts for bread sufficient to supply each workman with a pound per day, and saw that the value was regularly stopped from the men's wages at the end of the week. In the winter of 1810 and 1811, when the country was totally exhausted of provisions, this system was improved into a regular supply of a pound of biscuit per man issued by the British commissariat, for which three vintems per day were deducted from the wages of the peasantry.

Superintendence.—The number of officers of engineers employed on the lines never exceeded seventeen at the same time, viz. eleven British, two Hanoverian, and four Portugueze, and the number of their own soldiers never exceeded eighteen rank and file; but they had the assistance of more than 150 soldiers of the line, principally artificers, selected from the regiments at Lisbon. The latter were under the charge of a captain stationed at Mafra, and a subaltern at Alhandra, but were divided into parties of two and three each throughout the whole extent of the country to be retrenched.

In some of the districts a subaltern officer of engineers with that small number of English soldiers, utterly ignorant of the language, directed and controlled the labours of a thousand or fifteen hundred peasantry, compelled to work, many at the distance of forty miles from their homes, whilst their own lands lay neglected, and no Portugueze ever attended of higher authority than a cabo, equal, according to military classification, to a serjeant; nevertheless, during a twelvemonth of this forced labour, not a single instance of insubordination or riot occurred, and the great quantity of work performed should, in justice to the Portugueze, be more ascribed to regular habits of persevering labour in those employed, than to the efficiency of the control exercised over them.

Mode of Payment.—On commencing the lines, the officers of engineers were made public accountants, contrary to the regulations of the service, which strictly prohibit it, and they had, in consequence, to take charge of large sums of money (all in silver) and make the weekly payments of the labourers' wages.

Every moment of the engineers' time being devoted to the works, and no officer having a secure place to lodge the cash, nor any competent person to keep his accounts, many were considerable losers by this duty, and the active service of the senior officer of each district was altogether lost one day in the week whilst settling with the workmen, each of whom individually received and signed in triplicate for his 4*s.* 1¼*d.* which useless formality rendered the payment of 1,500 or 2,000 men the labour of many hours.

After some months, the impolicy as well as injustice of making the engineers paymasters becoming apparent, an officer of the commissariat, with efficient clerks, was named for that duty, and made a regular round of the districts, paying the workmen on lists prepared and certified by the engineers. In a similar manner during the latter periods of the war, in carrying on works in detached situations, the officer of engineers was relieved from the responsibility of being a public accountant, by the duty of paymaster being allotted to an ordnance clerk or conductor of stores, who received a sum of money to cover the intended service from the commissary-general, and disbursed it on the order of the engineer in charge of the work.

Materials, Stores, &c. how obtained.—All materials, stores, implements, &c. were purchased by the commissary-general on requisition from the commanding engineer, and the officers in charge of the several districts only gave receipts for the quantities delivered to them, being in no way responsible for or consulted respecting the price.

Lieut. Colonel Fletcher had a general authority from the commander of the forces to make these demands on the commissary-general, and when he gave over the charge of completing the lines to Captain John T. Jones, and made him responsible for the future expenditure, he also transferred his authority to order materials, &c., which authority so delegated was found efficient. In like manner, Captain Goldfinch was subsequently invested with similar delegated powers and responsibility, whilst retrenching the position of Almada; and generally speaking, each officer when employed in charge of a distinct work had authority to make demands on the nearest commissariat station.

The gunpowder, used for blasting during the formation of the scarps of the lines, the quantity of which was very considerable, also that used for mining the bridges and roads, was obtained from the ordnance commissary at Lisbon as wanted, on requisition addressed to the commanding officer of artillery.

When mining was ordered in situations distant from any artillery depôt, it was at first customary to draw cartridges from the nearest brigade of guns: but as this was invariably found to be a source of vexation to the artillery officers, a supply of gunpowder was latterly transported with the engineers' stores, with cases ready prepared for given charges.

Trace of the several works.—The redoubts were made of every capacity, from that of fig. 7, limited by want of space on the ground it occupied to 50 men and 2 pieces of artillery, to that of fig. 10, for 500 men and 6 pieces of artillery, the importance of the object to be attained being the only guide in forming the dimensions. Many of the redoubts first thrown up, even some of the smallest, were shaped like stars (Figs. 3 and 9), under the idea of procuring a flank defence for the ditches; but this construction was latterly rejected, it being found to cut up the interior space, and to be almost fallacious with respect to flank defence, the breadth of the exterior slopes being in some cases equal to the whole length of the flanks so obtained, as in fig. 9. Even when, from the greater size of the work, some flanking fire was thus gained, the angle formed by the faces was generally so obtuse, that it demanded more coolness in the defenders than ought reasonably to be expected, to aim along the ditch of the opposite face: and further, this construction prevented the fire of the work being more powerful in front than in rear.

In order to decide on the proper trace of a work, it is necessary to consider whether its object be to prevent an enemy establishing himself on the ground on which it is to be placed, or whether it be to ensure a heavy fire of artillery on some other point in its vicinity. In the first case, every consideration should be sacrificed to that of adding to its powers of self-defence, by flanks or other expedients. In the second, its powers of resistance are secondary to the establishment of a powerful offensive fire, and its trace cannot be too simple. Latterly, the shape of the redoubts was invariably that most fitted to the ground, (Figs. 4, 6, 10, 11, 12, 13, 14, 15,) or such as best parried the enfiladefire or musketry plunge of neighbouring heights, care being taken to present the front of fire deemed necessary towards the pass, or other object to be guarded; and such will generally be found the best rule of proceeding.

This recommendation, however, is not intended to apply to isolated works of large dimensions, and more particularly to those considered the key of any position. No labour or expense should be spared to render such works capable of resisting the most furious assault, either by breaking the parapet into flanks, or forming a flank defence in the ditch; for the experience gained in the Peninsula shows that an unflanked work of even more than an ordinary field profile, if skilfully and determinedly assaulted, will generally be carried—for instance, redoubt Renaud, forts Picurina and Napoleon, &c. Nor does the serious evil of curtailing the interior space, which renders any breaks in the outline to procure flanks so objectionable in small works, apply to works of large dimensions; for it must be recollected, that in similar figures, whilst the length of the outline increases only in the simple ratio of the double, triple or quadruple, the interior space or surface increases as the square of their like sides. Under this view, the great work on Monte Agraça (Fig. 2.) must be considered as very defective, the flank defence being confined to an occasional break of a few feet in the trace, caused by a change of direction in the contour of the height, whilst the interior space is more than doubly sufficient for the number of its allotted garrison to encamp.*

* It was understood at the moment, that General Junot strongly urged Marshal Massena to permit him to advance up the mountain with a division just before the dawn of day, and make a desperate effort to carry the large work by assault. This

Interior and other defences.—This work, however, had some of its most exposed salient points, or those most easy of access, or most likely to be assaulted, cut off by earthern lines of parapet, steeply reveted externally, and so traced as to serve for traverses to the interior. It had also three or four small inclosed posts formed within it; and the work at Torres Vedras, (Fig. 1.) had each of its salient points formed into an independent post. These interior defences and retrenchments were intended to guard against a general panic amongst the garrison, which would necessarily be composed in part of indifferent troops, and also to prevent the loss of the work by the entry of the assailants at any weak or ill-defended point. Such interior lines to rally on are absolutely essential to the security of a large field-work. They serve as substitutes for the block-house or tower, placed in the interior of all well constructed permanent earthen works, and merit

was good counsel abstractedly, and the assault would probably have been crowned with success, had the garrison been isolated; but there being a division of infantry bivouacked in rear of the heights, which was under arms every morning long before day-break, and had a ready communication all round the counter-scarp, they would have marched on the flank of the assailants on the first musket being fired, and have rendered the attempt abortive and highly destructive.

far more attention than they generally receive.

The small circular windmills of stone, which were frequently found occupying salient knolls selected for the site of advanced flèches, readily converted into admirable interior posts of that nature; and many mills situated on the elevated points of the main defences were made to add greatly to their security by a similar conversion. (Figs. 24, 25, and 26.)

Redoubt, No. 109, occupying a very important, and very exposed point in advance of the position of Oeyras, was deemed of so much value, that being commanded by a height between 6 and 700 yards in its front, in order to ensure some power of resistance after its parapet and scarps should have been destroyed, its artillery dismounted, and its interior plowed up by a cannonade from the height, a gallery, loop-holed for reverse flanking fire along the ditch, was formed behind the counterscarp at the salient angle of the front faces, and a communication made to it from the interior, under the bottom of the ditch. The soil being of a hard chalky substance, which stood without support, fixed the adoption of this means of defence in preference to the ordinary caponière, which requires so much less labour. (Figs. 11 and 23.)

The parapet of No. 109 was also cut en cremaillière to throw a musketry fire on the salient angle next the heights, and to screen the defenders of its left face from the enfilade fire of the heights. This mode of indenting the parapet, however, was not thought a good measure generally, it being found to add very much to the labour, and to abstract from the direct fire of the work, an equal quantity to that it threw in a different direction; besides making the defence of the parapet rather complex for militia. Therefore, latterly, in those redoubts where any particular trace was not imperious, it was always preferred to make an additional face to the work, than to leave a salient angle so acute as to necessitate such extra support; and at Almada, this principle was carried so far as to render the contour of some of the redoubts almost circular. (Figs. 14 and 15.)

Situations of the works.—Many of the redoubts were placed on very elevated situations on the summit of steep hills, which gave them a most imposing appearance; but it was in reality a defect highly prejudicial to their efficiency and defence, for the fire of their artillery on the object to be guarded became so plunging, as to lose half its powers; the musketry could not be made to scour the face of the hill sufficiently; and during the night both arms became of most uncertain effect.

The domineering situation of the redoubts, however, gave confidence to the young troops which composed their garrisons, protected them from a cannonade, and screened their interior from musketry, unless fired at a high angle, and consequently at random. These considerations perhaps justified the unusually elevated sites, selected for most of the redoubts on the lines, though they cannot induce an approval of them as a general measure. Indeed, the ill consequences arising from height of situation was so strongly felt on the lines, that on very elevated points, particularly at Monte Agraça, in order to command the face of the mountain, flèches, or small redoubts, were established in front of the main work, (Fig. 2.) on the projecting knolls, which afforded the best flanking points. These advanced batteries were made of the same strong profile in front as the redoubts, and their gorges were equally secured, except that the rear parapets, were formed as mere screens, so as not to give cover against the fire of the main work; and for the same object, the counterscarps of the rear ditches were sloped into the plane of the parapets of the commanding work. Even these flèches, though nearly doubling the garrison, saw the face of the hill less perfectly than the main work alone would have done, if placed on a height of a more moderate and more regular ascent, which shows that very elevated situations for works are seldom to be preferred.

At some points, where it was deemed likely that the troops would act in combination with redoubts occupying the summits of very elevated knolls, flèches, or field batteries, were prepared for the field brigades in the best flanking or enfilading situations, much lower down on the face of the hill. This seems the most judicious mode of occupying a height as a field position, when the artillery can be placed under the effectual musketry fire of the redoubt; but on these lines, it being impossible to foresee which part might or might not be occupied strongly by troops, it was made a rule to put no artillery in battery, except within works capable of defending themselves. At some points, where space could not be obtained within the redoubts, the guns were placed on a lower advanced level, connected on its flanks with the defences of the redoubt. (Fig. 8.) Some of the flank defences were limited to one or two guns, which could only be justified by the difficulty an enemy would find in passing the object they fired upon. It ought to be received as a general rule, that no flank can be formidable to infantry which does not contain at least three pieces of ordinance; and even to render a flank of three pieces very destructive, it must be in a situation of tedious approach, or in a work which cannot be run into.

Profiles.—The profile of the several works varied on every face and flank, according to its liability to be attacked or cannonaded, the only general rule enforced, being, that all ditches should be at least 15 feet wide at top and 10 feet in depth, and the crest of the parapet have at least five feet command over the crest of the counterscarp.

No parapet exceeded 10 feet in thickness, unless exposed to be severely cannonaded, and few more than 6 or 8 feet; and some, on high knolls, where artillery could not by any possibility be brought against them, were made of stone or rubble less than two feet in thickness, to gain more interior space, and allow full liberty for the use of the defenders' bayonets. Many of the rear enclosures, when supported on precipices, were merely screens; and in some few cases, on the position near Ribaldiera, they were left to the precipice itself. (Fig. 5.) The rear of advanced flèches and other small works, situated within good musketry-fire of the main defences, were generally closed with a very open but strong stockade. (Figs. 24, 25 and 26.)

In elevated situations, many of the banquettes were raised within four feet of the crest of the parapet, it being the rule to fix the level along each face at such height as would admit of the musketry plunging down the face of the hill, or at least seeing some yards of the glacis.

The exterior slopes were made greater or less, according to the tenacity of the soil; but it was found after the first winter, that no slope cut through the natural ground had sustained itself at a greater angle than 45°, and in made ground, the exterior slopes were washed away at that angle. Indeed, in consequence of the heavy rains in southern climates, it is almost essential to form some kind of revetment to works to keep them defensible during winter; and in 1811, most of the exterior slopes of the works of the lines were retained with dry stone walls. To ensure an efficient system of drainage should always be a principal consideration with an officer on commencing a work. Some redoubts deeply excavated, with the view to screen the defenders, particularly Nos. 101 and 102, at Oeyras, from neglect of this precaution, literally filled with water in September, 1810, and the labour of forming drains to keep their interior dry was little less than that of constructing the redoubt.

The interior of the parapets were retained with fascines or sand-bags: the former stood perfectly well, except that those originally made, being composed of the smaller branches and twigs, became, during the summer, so readily combustible as to be considered unsafe, and latterly, only the larger branches, completely divested of their leaves and twigs, were worked into fascines, intended for interior revetments. The sand-bags rotted and burst after the first winter.

A drawing is given of the profile of several of the works in different situations (Figs. 16 to 23); that of the redoubts, on the heights of Almada, (Fig. 20,) deserves particular attention, as those works stand in situations open to be violently cannonaded, and the hills forming the position are such as are most frequently occupied with works, and the profile was fixed after the experience gained in making the lines: it was as follows:—

	Feet.	In.
Height of interior crest of parapet	7	0
Height of parapet above banquette	4	3
Thickness of parapet	14	0
Berm	2	0
Breadth of ditch at top	16	0
Depth below surface of ground	12	0
Crest of glacis below crest of parapet	5	6

In the profile of lines of flanked works, in low situations, where the interior space was not limited, the crest of the parapet was generally fixed at 10 feet above the level of the ground, for the purpose of a better command in front, and better covering the troops; and this height was thought to be the best adapted for attaining a good defence with moderate labour. Even with this elevation, no covered way was formed to any line, but the crest of the glacis was kept six feet or six feet and a half below that of the parapet.

The redoubts of the lines being mostly thrown up as secure emplacements for guns, and to procure an open field for the fire of their artillery being the principal object attended to in their construction, they were mostly placed on the summit of the heights they occupied, so that each face might have a full command of the ground in its front, or of the point it was intended to protect; but, in other situations, where the object of a redoubt was merely to prevent an enemy occupying a particular spot, it was, wherever practicable, constructed on an inclined plane on the reverse of the height, so that only its most salient point, or, perhaps, its front faces, rose over the crest of the hill. (Fig. 22.) This defilement gives the work considerable protection from cannonade, and causes the front parapet to cover the rear lines and the defenders far better than if constructed on a horizontal plane, and should generally be adopted in situations where an enemy cannot establish batteries in its rear; and invariably in the construction of lunettes or flèches in advance of a fortress, as, beyond the advantages abovementioned, it causes the interior of the work to be completely seen from the place.

In this construction the rear enclosure, whether palisades or a wall, should be made of a strength to resist light howitzer shells pitched over the parapet, but not so strong as to afford cover against the heavy guns of the place.

Stores and provisions.—In each redoubt wholesome casks were provided and placed in security to contain four quarts of fresh water per man for the calculated garrison, besides the tubs with water for the use of the artillery; and a depôt of entrenching tools was also provided in the following proportions.

	Shovels.	Pickaxes.	Felling Axes.
Works for 400 men .	10	6	3
300 . . .	8	4	2
200 . . .	7	4	2
Smaller	6	3	2

Monte Agraça, proportion for 1500 men.

Magazines.—The magazines were formed of

splinter-proof timbers, about 10 inches by 8, placed at an angle between 45 and 50° against a substantial traverse; and wherever an efficient drain could be made around them, their floors were sunk one, two, three, and even four feet below the level of the interior of the work; which excavation, and the relative height of the redoubt with respect to the ground in its vicinity, served to regulate the length of the timber, so as to have the top of the magazine sheltered from direct fire.

The magazines were lined internally with plank, and strengthened externally with two feet of earth in sand bags, over which tarpaulins were spread, and thus protected, these magazines were found sufficiently dry.

Platforms.—The platforms, as originally laid down, consisted merely of a plank for each truck, but during the summer and autumn of 1810 they were all replaced by platforms of the ordinary construction. Many of the redoubts being on undulating heights, and the guns being mounted on extremely low carriages, it required undeviating attention to keep the front of the platform on a sufficiently high level to ensure the guns clearing the intermediate swell of the height, so as to strike an object at the foot of the slope. In such situations the eye will frequently attain an object which the gun on its lower level will not.

Palisades.—The palisades in the ditches were mostly young fir trees from four to five inches in diameter roughly pointed, and fixed three or four feet into the ground with a ribband very low down, and when the ditches were broad, much nearer the counterscarp than the scarp.

In the last campaign the palisades of the redoubts thrown up near the Montagne de la Couronne in the Pyrenees, where wood was plentiful and cost nothing, were made of trunks of trees placed close together at the foot of the escarpe, and were found almost equal to a masonry revetment.

The best disposition of the ordinary palisades in works with wide ditches was thought that adopted for the advanced redoubt, No. 109, at the position of Oeyras, Fig. 23, where they were fixed as fraises along the counterscarp, about two feet below its crest, with an inclination towards the bottom of the ditch. Fraises in that situation are little likely to be injured by a front fire of cannon or howitzers, and the manual operation of cutting them away is extremely difficult, besides the men, whilst so employed, being exposed to the fire from the parapet of the work. This mode of fixing fraises was also partially applied to some salient angles, on the approach to which little fire could be brought.

It should be observed, however, that fraises being much more liable to be broken down by vertical fire than palisades, are more adapted for field than reveted redoubts, as vertical fire can seldom be brought against the former, and it ought to form the basis of attack of the latter.

Barriers.—Each redoubt was closed with a barrier-gate, and a bridge of joists and planks.

For these four last-mentioned services more than 50,000 trees were received between the 7th July and 7th October, 1810; the greater part however being firs from the royal forests no payment was made for them.

Abattis.—The abattis were formed solely of the stems and boughs of whole trees well pointed, all the smaller branches being cut off, so that the front of the abattis afforded neither cover nor concealment to an assailant, although it presented a barrier of spears five, six, and seven feet in height. The abattis were usually placed from twenty to thirty yards in front of the work, each stem and large branch being firmly staked down into the ground, and when practicable, the trace was so disposed as to be flanked along its front by some of the defences.

Obstacles in this situation are undoubtedly the best means that can be devised for aiding the defence of works, and are seldom sufficiently attended to.

The great object of defence should be to contrive some expedient to check the assailants, and cause them to halt, if only for two or three minutes, under a close fire of musketry from the parapet. Such an advanced obstacle has ten times the effect of one of equal difficulty opposed to an assailant, when he has closed with the defenders of a work. He knows that in the latter case he has but to overcome one difficulty to obtain complete success, whereas in the former case the troops exhaust their ardour and lose their formation on a mere preliminary effort; and every one must have felt how extremely difficult it is to revive confident boldness, and restore order for a second effort after a check.

Fir trees were found the least, and Olive trees the best adapted to form abattis.

Trous-de-Loup.—The trous-de-loups were at first made of the ordinary dimensions and numbers, but subsequently an increased number of rows (eight or ten) of pits, only two feet or 2ft. 6in. in depth, well staked at bottom and in the intervening spaces, were considered preferable, as affording no cover within them for men to fire on the work, before which they might be placed, and presenting great impediments to the advance of an assailant.

During the occupation of the lines, trous-de-loups were formed in front of part of the position of Via Longa, consisting of a triple row of inverted cones, 9 or ten feet in diameter at top, and of the same depth.* These were found to be a most formidable obstacle, but were perhaps larger than absolutely required, as it is only necessary that trous-de-loups should be of a depth to prevent an assailant getting into them and firing over their tops, which 7 or 8 feet will effect.

Whenever practicable, from the height of the profile or the fall of the ground, the rows of trous-de-loups were concealed and protected from cannonade by forming an advanced glacis with the earth excavated from the pit.

Artillery.—The provision of artillery, ammunition and artillery stores was arranged by the Portugueze in the arsenal at Lisbon, on memo-

* By Captain Burgoyne.

randa sent from time to time by the commanding engineer, and the guns were mounted by parties of Portugueze gunners detached from thence, as the works were prepared to receive them. It was gratifying to observe, on these occasions, by what persevering and patient labour the peasantry, with their rude means of transport, (merely the common cars of the country pushed forward by oxen,) succeeded in transporting 12-pounders into situations where wheels had never before rolled, and along the steep sides of mountains where horses would have been useless.

Although the armament of the lines ultimately amounted to nearly double the number of pieces of ordnance originally contemplated, the zeal and perseverance of the Portugueze general Rosa smoothed all difficulties, and his activity and resource seemed to render the supply of guns, ammunition, and the means of transport, inexhaustible; and, highly to his credit, every thing supplied, though rude and inconvenient, proved efficient and substantially good. The Portugueze officers and gunners employed on this duty were also zealous and active, and took extremely good care of their stores and ammunition. Their numbers assembled on the lines amounted to 3,208, regulars and irregulars.

Calculation of garrisons.—As a general rule, the garrisons of the redoubts and the number of troops required to man the retrenchments were at the commencement calculated on an allotment of two men per yard running of parapet for all lines; but after some time, this calculation was deemed too considerable, and the numbers were fixed at two men per yard running for all front lines, and one man per yard for all rear lines, deducting for the spaces occupied by the artillery; an addition to or deduction from these numbers being made by the commanding engineer in all cases where deemed expedient from local causes.

Admitting each man to require three feet to enable him to use his musket freely, this latter calculation will, (whatever be the figure of the work,) ensure the parapet being sufficiently manned, and leave a reserve to supply the place of those killed, or in large works to charge the first of the assailants who may penetrate into the interior. It was therefore deemed preferable to the more scientific formula for allotting a man to a certain number of square feet of the interior space, which rule, though well calculated to apportion the garrison of every sized work in a similar ratio between its interior space and its length of parapet, seems too much the result of theory, which requires that each man of a garrison should have a certain space for his accommodation; whereas in practice such does not appear to be essentially necessary, for till the moment of being menaced with an attack, many of the garrison of each work will be kept on the watch on the face of the hill, and others be permitted to amuse themselves in its rear. All cooking, &c. is also performed outside of the work, so that it is only at night, or during the action which decides the fate of the position, that the garrisons are closely shut up, and then at least one third should be kept constantly standing or sitting under arms on the banquette. Besides this, every figure from the triangle to the circle varies in the proportion the content bears to the periphery, and it is on the latter only that the defence hinges.

Scarps.—The scarps were formed by cutting the front slopes of ranges of heights near their summit as perpendicularly as the soil or rock of which they were composed could be made to stand, or on such irregularity of level as presented the greatest facility for making a perpendicular cut.

The chief difficulty in tracing a line to be scarped was to find portions of the ascent sufficiently steep, that when cut to the required angle, the base should not form a road, which might serve as a breathing and rallying point, and unless flanked, a secure communication to an assailant. Fig. No. 27 is a section of a scarp of nearly two miles in length, formed along the summit of the front of the position of Alhandra, in August and Sept. 1810. Much of the upper twenty or thirty feet of that range of heights was found to be a ledge of precipitous rock only covered with a few feet of earth; which covering being removed and thrown down the face of the hill, the rock behind it was readily made insurmountable to infantry by means of blasting. At other points a species of sandstone, which, when cut through, stood nearly perpendicular, afforded great facility to the formation of the scarps; indeed, without some such natural aid, scarping will seldom be found practicable.

It never was presumed that scarps could be trusted to without defenders; but it was considered a great point gained to have rendered portions of ground of such difficult access as to be safely left to the guard of a small corps, or to unsteady troops, such as the militia and ordinanza, on the lines. For the purpose of better watching and to ensure the ready approach of troops and field artillery to all points of the front scarped, a line of interior road was formed nearly parallel to the scarps of Alhandra and Picanceira, at the shortest convenient distance from the front.

Roads and communications.—The military roads generally were traced along the rear of ranges of heights on the shortest line, concealed from the view of the ground in front; they were perfected during 1811, so as to form a ready communication along the front line from the sea to the Tagus, with direct communications from the rear line.

Several miles of the lateral road were entirely new, as also most of the direct communications from the lateral road to the works: but the intermediate communications between the advanced works and rear line were merely the original car roads of the country widened and rendered practicable for military purposes. Many of the communications along the valleys were of necessity paved to keep them in a state to be used; but generally the heights over which the main communication passed were rocky or abounded with loose stones and other materials which readily formed into firm roads. Fig. 21 is a section of the covered road commenced at Almada and intended to be carried from the right to the left of that position.

Telegraphs.—The telegraphs were composed

of a mast and yard, from which latter balls were suspended; the vocabulary used was that of the navy, many sentences and short expressions peculiar to the land service being added. These telegraphs readily communicated with each other, at the distance of seven and eight miles; but in consequence of the ranges of hills interrupting the view, it required five principal stations to communicate along the front line, viz. at Alhandra, Monte Agraça, N. S. de Socorra, Torres Vedras, and redoubt No. 30, in rear of Ponte de Rol.

The telegraphs were worked by a party of seamen under Lieutenant Leith of the Royal Navy.

Ground how obtained.—The ground required for the site of works, roads, abattis, scarps, &c. was taken possession of without a reference to or complaint from the owner or occupier, or any estimate being made of its value, which however was seldom considerable. Compensation was made to the proprietors for the olive trees cut down, also for trees felled in private woods, and for crops destroyed before the advance of the invaders. The owners of mills dismantled in consequence of being on knolls selected for the site of works had a monthly payment equivalent to their previous average gains, and also a sum of money for the restoration of the machinery; but otherwise, the principal injury sustained by private property being inflicted when the lines became the seat of war, the loss fell on individuals.

Conduct of the Portugueze.—The British officers of engineers, spread singly over a space of 150 square miles of country and billeting themselves in the best or most convenient houses, were every where treated with civility and kindness by the inhabitants; and a general readiness was shown by the upper classes to admit them to the familiar society of their families, which led to many sincere and disinterested friendships being contracted between individuals of the two nations. Indeed, it is but a tribute of justice to the Portugueze gentlemen and peasantry of Estramadura to state that, during many months of constant personal intercourse, both public and private, the latter ever showed themselves respectful, industrious, docile and obedient, whilst the former in every public transaction evinced much intelligence, good sense and probity, and appeared in their domestic relations, kind, liberal, and indulgent, both as masters and parents.

Secrecy with respect to the extent and nature of the works going forward was enjoined, and it is highly creditable to all concerned that scarcely a vague paragraph respecting the lines found its way into the public prints; and notwithstanding the magnitude of the works, the invaders remained ignorant of the nature of the barrier raising against them, till they found the army arrayed on it to stop their further advance.

Total of Retrenchments and Garrisons.—The length of retrenchment completed at the period the army occupied the lines, including the periphery of 126 enclosed works, when calculated on the data before mentioned, required 29,751 men for its defence, and there were mounted on it 427 pieces of artillery, independently of the works to cover an embarkation at St. Julian's, which were calculated for 5,350 men, and contained 94 pieces of artillery. It is however evident from the description of the lines that little more than a third part needed to be kept fully manned at the same period.

In 1812, when the lines were considered as perfect as they could be made, they consisted of 152 distinct works, armed with 534 pieces of ordnance, and required on the same calculation 34,125 men for their garrisons. The embarkation position remained as above described.

Expense of the Lines.—The disbursements on account of the lines, to the 6th July, 1810, were about £60,000; at the moment of the army occupying the ground the disbursements amounted to nearly £100,000: which sum was doubled before the conclusion of the war, by the outlay for the position of Almada, the repair and preservation of the various defences and communications, and by indemnities to some individuals for property wantonly destroyed or taken for the use of the troops during the occupation of the lines.

Public Mention made of the Lines.—" Having advanced from the positions in which I was enabled to bring the enemy to a stand and oblige them to retire without venturing upon any attack, it is but justice to Lieut. Colonel Fletcher and the officers of the Royal Engineers, to draw your Lordship's attention to the ability and diligence with which they have executed the works by which these positions have been strengthened to such a degree as to render any attack upon that line occupied by the allied army very doubtful, if not entirely hopeless. We are indebted for these advantages to Lieut. Colonel Fletcher and the officers of the Royal Engineers, among whom I must particularly mention Captain Chapman, who has given me great assistance upon various occasions."*— *Dispatch from Viscount Wellington, dated Cartaxo, Nov.* 21*st*, 1810.

* Captain Chapman was next in seniority to Lieut. Colonel Fletcher from the commencement of the lines, and was thus deservedly particularized for the great zeal and activity he displayed in aiding to carry into effect the plans of his commanding officer.

WORKS COMPOSING THE LINES,

AS NUMBERED ON THE GROUND AND ON THE PLAN.

District No. 1.

From the Tagus at Alhandra to No. 11, above Arruda Road, inclusive.

Nos. of the Works.	Infantry required.	Artillery mounted.				Names of Places where situated.
		12 Prs.	9 Prs.	6 Prs.	$5\frac{1}{2}$ How.	
1	1,000	4	3	6	..	Line across the low ground at Alhandra, resting on the Tagus.
2	800	2	..	..	..	Rising line to the left of do. do.
3	200	2	..	..	..	Redoubt, left extremity of rising line.
4	..	..	2	..	..	Right Flank to the scarped face of the position.
114	100	..	2	1	..	Flanking Redoubt to the scarped front of Alhandra.
115	100	..	2	..	..	do. do.
116	100	..	5	..	..	do. do.
117	150	..	..	..	..	Flèche do. do.
118	400	8	..	..	..	Redoubt on the most commanding point of the Alhandra position.
119	350	6	..	..	..	Redoubt closing the left of the position.
6	..	2	..	..	..	Barbette Battery retired on the extreme of the left.
120	130	2	..	..	..	Redoubt, extremity of left of front of the heights of Alhandra.
5	120	..	3	..	..	do. do.
121	250	..	3	1	..	Heights of Calhandrix, advanced redoubt
122	300	3	..	..	..	do. right.
123	300	3	..	..	..	do. centre.
124	350	3	1	..	..	do. left.
125	250	4	..	..	..	Rear Work, to connect the Calhandrix position with the rear line.
7	200	3	..	..	..	Redoubt on the heights in rear of Alhandra, looking up valley of Calhandrix.
			11	1	..	The valley of Calhandrix is closed at its mouth by a line of intrenchment and abattis, not numbered, thrown up whilst the army occupied the lines.
8	200	3	..	..	..	Heights in rear nf Trancoso de Cima, to prevent Alhandra being turned with artillery.
9	280	..	3	..	..	St. Sebastian, right of pass of Matos.
10	400	2	1	..	..	Carvalhao, left of the pass of Matos.
11	300	4	..	..	..	Moinho do Ceo. Windmill above Arruda road.
	6,280	51	36	9	..	

District No. 2.

From No. 12, above Arruda Road, to the Left of Monte Agraça.

Nos. of the Works.	Infantry required.	Artillery mounted.				Names of Places where situated.
		12 Prs.	9 Prs.	6 Prs.	5½ How.	
12	120	..	3	..	..	Forte do Passo, rocky bluff above Arruda road.
13	120	2	..	..	..	Forte de Canara, paved road leading to Bucellas.
14	1,590	14	6	4	1	Main work Monte Agraça.
15	460	3	3	1	..	Advanced work on the same hill.
16	250	1	2	..	1	do. do.
17	300	..	..	7	1	do. do.
152	250	4	2	..	..	Advanced work right of road leading to Sobral.
	3,090	24	16	12	3	

District No. 3.

From Zibriera to the Caduceira Heights, inclusive.

Nos. of the Works.	Infantry required.	Artillery mounted.				Names of Places where situated.
		12 Prs.	9 Prs.	6 Prs.	5½ How.	
151	300	..	..	..	..	Patameira, redoubt for field artillery. Scarped plateau between the Quinta de Anoteira and Ribaldeira prepared for field guns.
128	500	6	..	..	..	Large work Serra de Caduceira.
129	350	6	..	..	..	Centre do. do.
130	200	..	5	..	..	Left do. do.
28	270	3	..	..	..	Enxara dos Cavaleiros, north redoubt.
29	280	..	4	..	..	do. do. south redoubt.
	1,900	15	9	..	..	

District No. 4.

From No. 144, on the Left of the Pass of Runa, to the Sea.

	Nos. of the Works.	Infantry required.	Artillery mounted. 12 Prs.	9 Prs.	6 Prs.	$5\frac{1}{2}$ How.	Names of Places where situated.	
	149	250	4	2	..	..	Height above Matacaes, to command the Runa road.	
	26	300	..	3	..	..	Advanced mill near do. to block the Runa road.	
Main work, Torres Vedras.	20	470	5	..	2	1	S. E. Bastion of the main work at Torres Vedras.	1,720 men.
	21	270	..	2	6	1	S. W. do. do.	
	22	380	5	..	3	1	N. W. do. do.	
		600	..	..	..	..	South Curtain 150 men, W. Curtain 90, N. E. Curtain 360.	
	23	180	..	4	3	..	West Redoubt, Torres Vedras.	
	24	300	..	7	..	..	East Redoubt, Torres Vedras.	
	25	200	..	2	..	..	Convent of St. Joa.	
	27	500	5	..	..	..	Castle of Torres Vedras in the town.	
	131	90	4	..	..	..	Enclosed Battery, left of Variatoja.	
	132	150	6	..	..	..	do. left of do.	
	133	120	..	4	..	..	do. behind white Quinta.	
	134	110	4	..	..	..	do. ridge of Casal de Serra, overlooking the village and heights of Bemfica.	
	135	160	..	4	..	..	do. do.	
	136	150	4	..	..	..	do. do.	
	137	100	4	..	..	..	do. do.	
	147	..	..	..	..	..	Open Battery above Ponte do Rol.	
	148	..	..	..	..	..	do. do.	
	138	100	..	..	2	..	Enclosed Battery in rear of No. 30.	
	30	340	3	1	..	..	Redoubt above Ponte do Rol.	
	139	160	4	..	..	..	Enclosed Battery between Nos. 30 & 31.	
	140	120	4	..	..	..	do. do.	
	31	373	..	3	..	..	Redoubt at Algaterra.	
	141	180	4	..	..	..	Enclosed battery between 31 & St. Petro.	
	142	150	4	..	..	..	do. do.	
	143	150	..	4	..	..	do. do.	
	144	130	4	..	..	..	do. do.	
	32	260	3	1	..	..	At St. Pedro de Cadeira.	
	145	250	..	4	..	..	Quinta de Belmonte.	
	111	250	5	..	..	..	Between St. Pedro and the sea, Quinta de Passo.	
	146	250	..	6	..	..	Quinta de Bessuaria.	
	112	220	4	..	..	..	Between Quinta de Bessuaria & the sea.	
	113	50	2	..	..	..	Enclosed Barbette Battery at the sea.	
		7,413	78	47	16	3		

District No. 5.

From the Tagus to the Pass of Bucellas, inclusive.

Nos. of the Works.	Infantry required.	Artillery mounted.				Names of Places where situated.
		12 Prs.	9 Prs.	6 Prs.	$5\frac{1}{2}$ How.	
33	300	4	..	..	..	Banks of the Tagus, right of position of Via Longa.
34	200	..	3	..	..	Advanced Redoubt to enfilade Calçada, do.
35	120	..	4	..	..	do. do.
36	370	9	..	..	..	do. summit of advanced hill do.
37	50	..	3	..	..	Garden, right of paved road, do.
38	340	..	5	..	..	Building, left of road, do.
39	340	5	3	..	..	Summit of highest hill, do.
126	188	2	..	..	..	Right work to close the valley of Cabo.
127	154	..	..	..	..	Left do. do.
40	150	..	..	..	..	Caza de Portella, advanced redoubt. } These redoubts close the left of the position of Via Longa.
41	240	5	..	..	..	do. right.
42	350	6	..	..	..	do. left.
43	..	4	..	..	..	Right of Pass of Bucellas, open battery.
44	..	..	2	..	..	do. front emplacement.
45	..	3	..	..	..	do. rear do.
46	..	..	2	..	..	Left of Pass of Bucellas, front do.
47	..	3	..	..	..	do. rear do.
48	200	2	..	..	..	In rear of the Pass enfilading the Calçada.
18	300	4	..	..	..	Right work, Serra de Santa Ajuda.
19	200	..	3	..	..	Left do. do.
	3,502	47	25	..	..	

District No. 6.

From the Pass of Freixal to the Park of Mafra, including the Pass of Montachique.

Nos. of the Works.	Infantry required.	Artillery mounted.				Names of Places where situated.
		12 Prs.	9 Prs.	6 Prs.	$5\frac{1}{2}$ How.	
49	..	2	..	..	..	Pass of Freixal, emplacement right.
50	160	..	2	..	..	do. right redoubt.
51	300	4	..	..	..	do. left redoubt.
52	190	..	3	..	..	Right of the Pass of Montachique, entrance of Pass.
53	230	..	2	..	..	do. near the village of Prezenhiro.
54	210	..	..	..	..	do. mill on Euxara road.
55	150	3	..	..	..	do. rocky bluff.
56	150	2	..	..	..	do. pine wood.
57	270	3	..	..	..	do. rocky height covering the right.
58	310	..	3	..	..	Left of Pass of Montachique, entrance of Pass.
59	260	4	..	..	..	do. mill on Mafra road.
60	150	..	2	..	..	do. flèche covering the left flank.
61	190	..	2	..	..	do. covering the left flank.
62	390	3	..	..	..	In front of the road from Mafra to Montachique, covering the great road, Alto de Cheixa.
63	280	..	3	..	..	do. Cazal de Serra.
64	210	..	3	..	..	do. corner of park wall.
65	270	3	..	..	..	Mafra road, Oiteira de Sta. Maria.
66	350	4	..	..	..	do. Malveira.
67	120	..	2	..	..	do. right of 66.
68	260	4	..	..	..	do. Monte de Zinho.
69	240	4	..	..	..	do. Pinhal de Fidalgo.
70	240	4	2	..	..	do. Quinta de Estrangeiro.
71	240	..	4	..	..	do. do.
72	130	..	2	..	..	do. Astadieros.
73	340	3	..	..	..	do. Cazal de Conto.
	5,640	43	30	..	..	

District No. 7.

From the Park at Mafra, inclusive, to the Sea.

Nos. of the Works.	Infantry required.	Artillery mounted. 12 Prs.	9 Prs.	6 Prs.	$5\frac{1}{2}$ How.	Names of Places where situated.
74	190	..	2	..	..	Pass of Mafra, Cazal de Pedra, right of Park, within the entrance. } Right of Pass of Mafra.
75	70	..	2	..	..	Within walls of Park, advance Milharica. } Right of Pass of Mafra.
76	390	4	..	..	..	Cabeça de Sincout. } Right of Pass of Mafra.
77	380	4	..	..	..	Juncal. } Right of Pass of Mafra.
78	110	2	1	..	..	Serra de Chypre, advanced work.
79	270	3	..	..	..	redoubt, advanced mill.
80	310	3	..	..	..	second mill.
81	280	..	3	..	..	lower work.
82	210	2	2	..	..	Left of the village of Morugeira, right.
83	240	..	3	..	..	do. centre.
84	290	3	..	..	..	do. left.
85	290	3	..	..	..	Ereceira road to Mafra, Alto de Arriero.
86	280	3	..	..	..	do. Alto de Paz.
87	340	3	..	..	..	Mill, south of Ereceira road, Pinheiro.
88	200	3	..	..	..	To command the road from Sobral des Alarves to Mafra.
89	310	3	..	..	..	Defence of Picanceira road.
90	230	3	..	..	..	Peneyaixo, to command the roads leading from Picanceira and Encarnaçoa.
91	200	3	..	..	..	Lagoa, do. three roads leading from Encarnaçoa.
92	180	3	..	..	..	Defence of the road to Morvao.
93	330	3	..	..	..	Riba-mar, right.
94	320	2	..	..	..	do. left.
95	250	2	..	..	..	Rear line, right, Monte Gordo.
96	280	3	..	..	..	centre, Carvoiera.
97	350	2	..	..	..	left, St. Julian's.
	6,300	57	13	..	..	

District of Oeyras.

Nos. of the Works.	Infantry required.	Artillery mounted.					Names of Places where situated.
		24 Prs.	12 Prs.	9 Prs.	6 Prs.	$5\frac{1}{2}$ How.	
98	1,340	20	..	..	6	..	Main Work.
99	70	..	6	..	..	..	Right Battery to flank the valley and beach of Oeyras.
100	50	..	6	..	..	..	Left Battery to flank the valley of Oeyras.
101	250	..	10	..	..	..	Advanced to Great Work, right.
102	260	..	8	..	..	..	do. left.
103	130	..	..	3	..	..	Advanced in front of Oeyras, front.
104	100	..	..	2	..	..	do. south mill.
105	170	..	..	4	..	..	do. north mill.
106	320	..	6	..	..	..	Vineyard left of 98.
107	800	..	6	..	..	..	Quinta Nova, building & redoubt.
108	360	..	6	..	..	..	Left flank of Position.
109	500	..	..	7	..	1	Advanced on a hill to the N. E. of Oeyras.
110	1,000	..	..	3	..	..	Line extending on the right from No. 104 to fort das Mais.
	5,350	20	48	19	6	1	

1st *May*, 1812.

***DETAIL** of the Number of Works, Troops, and Ordnance, as proposed originally for the Occupation of the Position of Almada. This project was subsequently reduced, as described in page 45.*

Works.	*Guns.*	*Men.*
Redoubt No. 1.	4	150
Redoubt No. 2.	4	150
Flèches and Outposts	2	100
Village of Morfacem	8	600
Redoubt No. 3.	4	200
Quinta de Geddos		50
Redoubt No. 4.	3	150
Redoubt No. 5.	5	250
Adjacent Village and Buildings		100
Redoubt No. 6.	12	600
Redoubt No. 7.	4	150
Adjacent Buildings		50
Redoubt No. 8.	5	150
Adjacent Village and Buildings		100
Redoubt No. 9.	5	200
Flèche and Village		100
Redoubt No. 10.	5	200
Adjacent Village		80
Redoubt No. 11.	5	250
Adjacent Roads and Buildings		100
Redoubt No. 12.	4	150
Flèche		50
Redoubt No. 13.	6	300
Adjacent Buildings		50
Redoubt No. 14.	4	150
Redoubt No. 15.	3	150
Flèche	2	50
Vill. N. Senora de Monte	6	400
Redoubt No. 16.	4	200
Redoubt No. 17.	5	200
Adjacent Buildings		60
Carried up	100	5,490

Works.	*Guns.*	*Men.*
Brought up	100	5,490
Redoubt No. 18.	5	200
Adjacent Buildings		60
Redoubt No. 19.	4	200
Flèche and Buildings	2	100
Redoubt No. 20.	6	300
Redoubt No. 21.	5	200
Adjacent Buildings		100
Redoubt No. 22.	3	150
Adjacent Buildings		40
Redoubt No. 23.	5	200
Flèche		40
Redoubt No. 24.	4	150
Adjacent Buildings		80
Redoubt No. 25.	4	150
Redoubt No. 26.	4	150
Flèche		40
Village of Pregal	4	300
Redoubt No. 27.	5	200
Redoubt No. 28.	4	150
Redoubt No. 29.	6	300
Redoubt No. 30.	5	200
Street and Buildings		150
Redoubt No. 31.	6	200
Redoubt No. 32.	4	150
Redoubt No. 33.	3	150
Redoubt No. 34.	3	200
Redoubt No. 35.	3	150
Village of Cazilhas		150
Town and Castle of Almada	12	800
TOTAL	197	10,750
RESERVE		4,000

No plan is given of the positions of Almada, Oeyras, or Setuval, as it is possible they may, in the course of years, be again occupied; and a reference can be made by those desirous of it to the plans in the office in London.

NOTES.

Note 1.

(Reference, page 3.)

The following paper of memoranda or instructions, given to Lieutenant-Colonel Fletcher for his guidance in proposing the mode of strengthening the ground in front of Lisbon, is extremely interesting as showing the first conceptions of a system of defence subsequently perfected into the lines of Torres Vedras.

Memorandum. Lisbon, *October* 20, 1809.

In considering the relative state of the strength and efficiency of the allied and French armies in the Peninsula, it does not appear probable that the enemy have it in their power to make an immediate attack upon Portugal. They must wait for their reinforcements, and as the arrival of them may be expected, it remains to be considered, what plan of defence shall be adopted for this country.

The great object in Portugal is the possession of Lisbon and the Tagus, and all our measures must be directed to that object. There is another also connected with that first object, to which we must likewise attend, viz. the embarkation of the British troops in case of a reverse.

In whatever season the enemy may enter Portugal, he will probably make his attack by two distinct lines, the one north the other south of the Tagus, and the system of defence to be adopted must be founded upon this general basis.

In the winter season the river Tagus will be full, and will be a barrier to the enemy's enterprises with his left attack, not very difficult to be secured. In the summer season, however, the Tagus being fordable in many places between Abrantes and Salvatierra, and even lower than Salvatierra, care must be taken that the enemy does not, by his attack directed from the south of the Tagus and by the passage of that river, cut off from Lisbon the British army engaged in operations to the northward of the Tagus. The object of the Allies should be, to oblige the enemy, as much as possible, to make his attack with concentrated corps. They should stand in every position which the country could afford such a length of time as would enable the people of the country to evacuate the towns and villages, carrying with them or destroying all articles of provisions and carriages not necessary for the allied army; each corps taking care to preserve its communication with the others, and its relative distance from the point of junction.

In whatever season the enemy's attack may be made, the whole allied army, after providing for the garrisons of Elvas, Almeida, Abrantes and Valença, should be divided into three corps, to be posted as follows: one corps to be in the Beira; one to be in the Alemtejo; and the third, consisting of the Lusitanean Legion, eight battalions of Chasseurs and one of Militia, in the mountains of Castello Branco.

In the winter the corps in the Beira should consist of two-thirds of the whole numbers of the operating army. In the summer the corps in the Beira and in Alemtejo should be nearly of equal numbers. I will point out in another memorandum the plan of operations to be adopted by the corps north and south of the Tagus in the winter months.

In the summer it is probable, as I have before stated, that he will make his attacks in two principal corps, and that he will also push on through the mountains between Castello Branco and Abrantes. His object will be by means of his corps south of the Tagus to turn the positions which might be taken in his front on the north of that river; to cut off from Lisbon the corps opposed to him; and to destroy it by an attack in front and rear at the same time. This can be avoided only by the retreat of the right, centre and left of the allies, and their junction at a point at which, from the state of the river, they cannot be turned by the passage of the Tagus by the enemy's left.

The first point of defence which presents itself below that at which the Tagus ceases to be fordable, is the river of Castenheira, and here the army should be posted as follows:—

Ten thousand able men, including all the cavalry, in the plain between the Tagus and the hills; 5,000 infantry on the hill to the left of the plain; and the remainder of the army, with the exception of the following detachments, on the height in front and on the right of Cadafoes.

In order to prevent the enemy from turning by their left the positions which the allies may take up for the defence of the high road to Lisbon by the Tagus,

Torres Vedras should be occupied by a corps of 5,000 men, the heights in the rear of Sobral de Monte Agraça by 4,000 men, and Aruda by 2,000.

There should be a small corps on the height east by south of the heights of Sobral, to prevent the enemy from marching from Sobral to Aruda; and there should be another small corps on the heights of Ajuda, between Sobral and Bucellas.

In case the enemy should succeed in forcing the corps at Torres Vedras, or Sobral de Monte Agraça, or Aruda. If at the first, it must fall back gradually to Cabeça de Montachique, occupying any defencible point on the road. If the second, it must fall back upon Bucellas, destroying the road over the height of . If the third, it must fall back upon Alhandra, disputing the road, particularly at a point one league in front of that town.

In case any one of these three positions should be forced, the army must fall back from its position as before pointed out, and must occupy one as follows:—

Five thousand men, principally light infantry, on the hill behind Alhandra; the main body of the army on the Serra of Serves, with its right on that part of the Serra which is near the Casal de Portella, and is immediately above the road which crosses the Serra from Bucellas to Alverca; and its left extending to the pass of Bucellas. The entrance of the pass of Bucellas to be occupied by the troops retired from Sobral de Monte Agraça, &c.; and the Cabeça de Montachique by the corps retired from Torres Vedras.

In order to strengthen the several positions, it is necessary that different works should be constructed immediately, and that arrangements and preparations should be made for the construction of others. Accordingly I beg Colonel Fletcher as soon as possible to review the several positions.

1. He will examine particularly the effect of damming up the mouth of the Castanheira river, how far it will render the river a barrier, and what extent it will fill.

2. He will calculate the labour required for that work, and the time it will take, as well as the means of destroying the bridge over the river, and of constructing such redoubts as might be necessary on the plain, and on the hill on the left of the road, effectually to defend the plain. He will state particularly what means should be prepared for these works. He will also consider of the means and time required, and the effect which might be produced by scarping the banks of the river.

3. He will make the same calculations for the works to be executed on the hill in front, and on the right of Cadafoes; particularly on the left of that hill, to shut the entry of the valley of Cadafoes.

4. He will examine and report upon the means of making a good road of communication from the plain across the hills with the valley of the Cadafoes and the left of the proposed position, and calculate the time and labour it will take.

5. He will examine the road from Otta Abringola, Labougeira to Merciana, and thence to Torres Vedras; and also from Merciana to Sobral de Monte Agraça. He will also examine and report upon the road from Alemquer to Sobral de Monte Agraça.

6. He will entrench a post at Torres Vedras for 5,000 men. He will examine the road from Torres

Vedras to Cabeça de Montachique, and fix upon the spots at which to break it up might stop or delay the enemy; and if there should be advantageous ground at such spots, &c. will entrench a position for 4000 men, to cover the retreat of the corps from Torres Vedras.

7. He will examine the position of Cabeça de Montachique, and determine upon its line of defence, and upon the works to be constructed for its defence by a corps of 5,000, of which he will estimate the time and labour.

8. He will entrench a position for 4,000 on the two heights which command the road from Sobral de Monte Agraça to Bucellas. He will entrench a position for 400 men on the height of St. Ajuda, between Sobral and Bucellas, to cover the retreat of the corps from Sobral to Bucellas; and he will calculate the means and the time it will take to destroy the road at that spot.

9. He will construct a redoubt for 200 men and three guns at the windmill on the height bearing east by south and east south-east from the height of Sobral de Monte Agraça; which guns will bear upon the road from Sobral to Aruda.

10. He will ascertain the points at which and the means by which the road from Sobral to Aruda can be destroyed.

11. He will ascertain the time and labour required to entrench a position which he will fix upon for 2,000 men, to defend the road coming out of Aruda towards Villa Franca and Alhandra.

12. He will fix upon the spots at which the road from Aruda to Alhandra can be destroyed with advantage.

13. He will construct a redoubt on the hill which commands the road from Aruda, about one league in front of Alhandra.

14. He will examine the little rivers at Alhandra, and see whether by damming them up at the mouths he could increase the difficulties of a passage by that place; and he will ascertain the time, labour and means which this work will require.

15. He will fix upon the spots and ascertain the time and labour required to construct redoubts upon the hill of Alhandra on the right, and prevent the passage of the enemy by the high road, and on the left, and in the rear, to prevent by their fire the occupation of the mountains towards Alverca.

16. He will determine upon the works to be constructed on the right of the position upon the Serra de Serves, as above pointed out, to prevent the enemy from forcing that point; and he will calculate the means and the time required to execute them. He will likewise examine the pass of Bucellas, and fix upon the works to be constructed for its defence, and calculate the means, time and labour required for their execution.

17. He will calculate the means, time and labour required to construct a work upon the hill on which a windmill stands, at the southern entrance of the pass of Bucellas.

18. He will fix upon the spots on which signal-posts can be erected upon these hills to communicate from one of these positions to the other.

19. It is very desirable that we should have an accurate plan of this ground.

20. Examine the island in the river opposite Alhandra, and fix upon the spot and calculate the means and

time required to construct batteries upon it and play upon the approach to Alhandra.

21. Examine the effect of damming up the river which runs by Loures, and calculate the time and means required to break the bridge at Loures.

WELLINGTON.

Upon the letter of these instructions the position of Castenheira, thirty-two miles in front of Lisbon, was commenced to be retrenched on the 8th January, 1810; but Lord Wellington, on a second personal reconnoissance of the ground on the 10th February following, perceiving that it was a line open to be turned, ordered the works to be filled in.

NOTE 2.

(Reference, page 17.)

VISEU, *February* 18, 1810.

SIR,

As the works carrying on under Lieutenant-Colonel Fletcher may require the employment of persons in the country, and the use of materials, without waiting for the employment of those persons, or the purchase of those materials by an officer of the Commissariat, I have to request that all orders for workmanship, labour or materials, drawn by Colonel Fletcher upon the Deputy Commissary-General at Lisbon, may be paid; Colonel Fletcher being held accountable for the money.

I have also to request that the Deputy Commissary-

General at Lisbon may be directed to supply Lieutenant-Colonel Fletcher with such numbers of fascines, palisades and picquets as he may require at such stations as he may point out, without waiting for further orders from me.

(Signed) WELLINGTON.

The Commissary-General,
&c. &c. &c.

NOTE 3.

(Reference, page 30.)

MEMORANDUM *sent to Lisbon during the Retreat of the Army.*

WITH a view to occupation of the works in the lines in the front of Lisbon, they must be divided into certain districts, and an officer must be appointed to command or regulate the troops in each. The troops (that is to say, the Militia, the British and Portugueze Artillery, and the Ordinança Artillery) must be assembled in the district; and the officer commanding, or the regulating officer, must make the arrangement and distribution of them, to be carried into execution when it will be necessary by the advance of the enemy.

The Commissary-General of the British army must supply all the troops in these positions under the arrangement of June, 1809; and there must be a Commissary in each district.

No. 1. . . Tents for 2,500 men.
No. 2. . . Tents for 2,000 men.
No. 3. . . Tents for 5,000 men.

No. 4. . . Tents for 5,000 men.
No. 5. . . Tents for 10,000 men.
No. 6. . . Tents for 10,000 men.

No. 1 District.—Troops to be assembled at the head-quarters forthwith.

2,470 Militia Infantry.
250 Ordinança Artillery.
140 Regular Portugueze Artillery.
70 British Artillery.

No. 2 District.—Troops to be assembled at the head-quarters forthwith.

1,300 Militia Infantry.
300 Artillery of Ordinanças.
140 Portugueze Artillery of the Line.
40 British Artillery.

No. 3 District.—Troops to be assembled at the head-quarters forthwith.

400 Militia Infantry.
60 Artillery of Ordinanças.
60 British Artillery.

No. 4 District.—Troops to be assembled at the head-quarters forthwith.

1,100 Militia Infantry.
500 Ordinança Artillery.
80 Portugueze Artillery of the Line.

No. 5 District.—To be assembled immediately.

2,400 Militia Infantry.
480 Ordinança Artillery.
120 Portugueze Artillery.
50 British Artillery.

No. 6 District.—Troops to be assembled at the head-quarters immediately.

700 Militia Infantry.
350 Ordinança Artillery.
230 Artillery of the Line.
40 British Artillery.

The Districts are to be as follows:—

No. 1. From Torres Vedras to the sea. Head-quarters, Torres Vedras.

No. 2. From Sobral de Monte Agraça to the valley of Calhandrix. Head-quarters, Sobral de Monte Agraça.

No. 3. From Alhandra to the valley of Calhandrix. Head-quarters, Alhandra.

No. 4. From the banks of the Tagus, near Alverca, to the Pass of Bucellas inclusive. Head-quarters, Bucellas.

No. 5. From the Pass of Freixal, inclusive, to the right of the Pass of Mafra. Head-quarters, Montachique.

No. 6. From the Pass of Mafra to the sea. Head-quarters, Mafra.

W.

NOTE 4.

(Reference, page 31.)

THE following is a copy of the letter of instructions under which the officers of Engineers acted as regulating officers in the several districts.

HEAD-QUARTERS, RIO-MAIOR,
6th October, 1810.

SIR,

I enclose a memorandum, by which you will see the manner in which I have divided into districts the country which has been fortified between the Tagus and the sea, the objects for which this division has been made, and that you are appointed regulating officer of the district No. —.

I likewise enclose a list of the redoubts and works in that district, stating the number with which each is marked, the number of guns it contains, and the number of infantry deemed necessary for the defence of each.

The business of your situation as regulating officer of district No. —, is to arrange the troops in their several stations when they will be sent into the district to occupy the redoubts; to take charge of the mines intended to blow up the roads and bridges; and to carry my orders in the district into execution till an officer to command the troops within it will be appointed; you are then to assist him in making his arrangements as one of his staff, and in the defence of his post, with your professional abilities.

(Signed) WELLINGTON.

Captain ———, Royal Engineers.

Note 5.

(Reference, page 63.)

In appreciating this distance of seven miles, it should be recollected that the number of men required to guard a position depends less on the extent of its front than on the facility of access to the several portions of it. Large armies with their numerous trains of artillery cannot engage across a country, particularly when the defensive force is strongly posted or retrenched; but their principal columns of attack must march by the great roads or open spaces. To ensure a victory over good troops, it is not sufficient to push up their position bodies of light and unsupported troops, or even strong columns with bayonets only, as Marshal Massena did at Busaco; but a superiority of force of all arms must be brought to act conjointly on the point destined to be overwhelmed.

Being so, it is evident that the nature and number of the lateral communications within, and of the direct and lateral communications without a position, are main points on which the force necessary for its occupation depend. In front of the range of heights extending from Monte Agraça to Torres Vedras, the only exterior road parallel to its front (that of Runa) was blocked to an offensive force till after the capture of several strong redoubts; and only two direct roads, and those little distant from each other, lead over the range. This ground consequently possessed defensive capabilities which far more than counterbalanced its extent of front.

APPENDIX.

THE following Letters and Extracts of Letters, which passed between Lieut. Colonel Fletcher and Captain Jones during the period the latter officer was charged with completing the Lines, are added to show the feelings and proceedings of the moment and to elucidate some portions of the text. They are also added from a wish to bear honourable tribute to the character of the late Sir R. Fletcher, whose correspondence evinces knowledge blended with diffidence, and command exercised through kind and friendly communication.

INSTRUCTIONS

FROM

LIEUTENANT COLONEL FLETCHER

TO

CAPTAIN JOHN T. JONES.

Mafra, *6th July*, 1810.

SIR,

As you will be left in the immediate charge of the engineer department in this part of Portugal,* I beg to call your attention to the following objects. As you find the works completed, and as you think the officers can be spared, I request you will employ them in making accurate surveys of the different positions.

You will, I imagine, soon find it practicable to part with a proportion of the men of the line now employed in the department, and they will then be sent to Lisbon; but I think some of the men should be kept to destroy bridges and roads at the last moment. I conceive you will shortly have it in your power to dispense with the services of the Figueiras and Torres Vedras

* This Letter accompanied a copy of the corps orders of the same date, printed as a note to page 21 of this pamphlet.

regiments of militia, and I request you will report when you can do so.

I beg you will also let me know when you think the services of the Portugueze engineers are no longer required. You will also please to report to me when all the artillery and ammunition for our different works are complete. From the description of the carriages it is desirable you should improve the platforms as materials can be procured for them; and as magazines not lined with boards are said to be less dry than those boarded, I request you will, as far as possible, have them completed with linings.

I wish to leave the mode of conducting the service generally entirely to your judgment. You are, I believe, perfectly aware of what is intended in the different districts, and the officers are severally acquainted with the details. I request you will report to me from time to time, and that you will make such observations as may appear necessary for the good of the service.

(Signed) R. FLETCHER.

Peniche, *7th July*, 1810.

I OBSERVE by a letter from Captain Burgoyne that engineers are much wanted at Fort Conception, and I therefore request you will order Lieut. Thomson to join the army, and let some other officer take charge of his works at Ponte de Rol.

Alverca da Beira, 14*th July*, 1810.

SIR,

THE Commander of the Forces has directed that the work on the hill above Oeyras, of which we have already spoken, should be thrown up. I think it should be for 400 or 500 men, and not less that six 12-pounders, and that it should be in every way respectable, and of a description not to be carried by assault. I request, therefore, that you will have the goodness to demand an additional number of workmen, and that you will commence it as soon as possible. The ammunition for the different works may continue in the nearest depôts for the present.

I am, &c.

Alverca da Beira, 17*th July*, 1810.

SIR,

THE Commander of the Forces has expressed a wish that the position of Alhandra should be strengthened as far as possible, whether by scarping or works, and I have therefore to request that you will examine that ground, and that you will cause redoubts to be commenced on such parts as may afford good flanking points, and as may appear to be at the same time favourable for the construction of enclosed works. They should, I conceive, have a ditch not less than 10 feet deep and 15 feet wide, and if the scarp will stand it, a slope that will render the work secure from assault. The bottom of the ditch should be palisaded. Should you find parts of the height that are favourable for scarping, you will employ a body of workmen upon them to render those places impracticable. His Lordship is also desirous that two or three good redoubts should be established between the work at S. Pedro de Cadiera and the sea. I think you will find one good situation at a hill about halfway between No. 32 and the sea, one near the sea, and a third at a point at which there was to have been a dam made. They should not, I conceive, be for less than 200 men, and three or four pieces of artillery each. You will probably find it convenient to keep the militia some time longer in consequence of these new works, but I will leave such arrangements entirely to you.

I am, Sir, &c. &c.

(Confidential Note inclosed in the above.)

My dear Sir,

In consequence of the new works you will probably hardly find it convenient to part with Captain Williams, but on this you will do as you please. With respect to the position at Alhandra, of course, nothing more can be expected than that some of the most prominent points should be taken to *assist* the defence, but Lord Wellington is anxious that as much as possible should be done there. The point at the mill, and that near the sea, are two striking features on the left of St. Pedro da Cadeira, and I think there is a third, though, probably, it may be as well to take up the two last first, but this you will decide on the spot. There was a difficulty about powder for blasting, and Lord Wellington will order General Howarth to issue whatever we may want, to my order; you had, therefore, better use my name in drawing it.

Alverca da Beira, 23*d* *July*, 1810.

My dear Sir,

I this morning received your three letters of the 18th. I am sorry to learn so bad an account of the signal posts; we thought that from any one of them to the next nearest, the balls would be very visible, and I am inclined to believe the principal fault lies in the telescopes, and I feel confident there will be no objection to your purchasing others of a better description, if you can find them. I am very glad to hear so good an account of works 86, 90, and 91. In consequence of the new works, about which I wrote to you on the 18th instant, I shall not report to head-quarters that the services of the Figuieras regiment of militia can be dispensed with till I hear further from you.

Alverca da Beira, 26th *July*, 1810.

P. S.—I THINK it will be advisable to improve the trenches on the right of the Alhandra position; at least, those on the left of the left of the road sloping up the hill. I am very glad that you found an expedient to avoid interfering with the salt-pans near Via Longa.

(Confidential.)

Head-quarters, Celorico, 29*th July*, 1810.

MY DEAR SIR,

As we seem now to have commenced our march towards your part of Portugal, I think it right to apprize you of it, that every thing on our different works may be in a state for immediate service. With respect to those lately commenced, you will naturally put them into such a state as at least to afford cover against musketry, and if the ditches are not of themselves sufficient impediments to an enemy, I think the bottom of them should, if possible, be palisaded; and you will, I am sure, generally have recourse to such obstructions as may occur to you on the spot. You can, I think, prepare these works for immediate service without interrupting their progressive improvement. You can close the entrances with a double row of our own chevaux-de-frize, unless any better method which you have the means of effecting should strike you. You will naturally prepare the magazines for the reception of the ammunition. The Commander of the Forces does not think it necessary that the abattis on the right of the Serra de Serves, or in any other places in which they may be ultimately useful, should be felled. I would, however, recommend your examining your depôts of felling axes, and the state of those tools. Lieut. Stanway can explain to you that the embankment in front of the redoubt on the Tagus (or the right of the Serra de Serves) and another on the bank of the river, were finally to be levelled, but not at this moment. It seems, I think, now desirable that Lieut. Leith should be in possession of the signal books.

Yours, &c.

Celorico, 31*st July*, 1810.

Sir,

I have this morning received your letter of the 25th, relative to the position at Alhandra.

I am very glad to find you can strengthen its front so materially by scarping, and I think the two redoubts for the further protection of the left very desirable. I therefore request that you will proceed upon these works with all possible despatch, and I am of opinion that it would be even advisable to begin the redoubts by withdrawing a part of the men employed in scarping, unless you can assemble a sufficient body to render such a step unnecessary.

Yours, &c.

Celorico, 3*d August*, 1810.

By a letter from Marshal Beresford, I learn that the Portugueze have been ordered to prepare a large quantity of hand grenades, which will be issued to your order. You are aware of the distribution for our works generally and for those lately undertaken, I beg you will decide.

Lord Wellington seems desirous that Captain Williams should join General Leith's corps as soon as the work on Monte Agraça is sufficiently advanced to admit of your sparing him with tolerable convenience.

Celorico, *10th August*, 1810.

I FEEL truly obliged and gratified by your satisfactory communication of the 3d instant; it eased my mind of much anxiety. I should think the works covering Setuval must be nearly completed; in that case, do you consider Captain Dickinson as disposable for any other service, or would it be more desirable to employ him on the works at St. Julian?

I request that when you think Captain Williams can be conveniently spared, you will order him to join Major General Leith.

Celorico, *12th August*, 1810.

LORD Wellington is very anxious to have the Figueiras regiment disposable, and he desired me to write to you to say if they could with tolerable convenience be spared he wished they might be allowed to go home; you will judge of this, and if you think they can be parted with, I will trouble you to say so to their immediate commanding officer.

Celorico, 14*th August*, 1810.

I HAVE received a letter from Mr. Pickering, wishing to know how I would dispose of the assistant-commissary clerk of stores and two conductors, expected from England, to be attached exclusively to the engineer department. I have said, that, for the present, I wish them to be placed at your disposal, and you will employ them as the service demands.

I will trouble you to ascertain whether the whole quantity of ammunition demanded for our different works has been supplied by General Rosa; a great deal remained to be sent forward when I left Lisbon.

On considering our works near Fort St. Julian, it at one time struck me that it would, if practicable, be desirable to connect the redoubts on the left by a common trench, in which bodies of troops might be placed in security from a cannonade, who could support the intervals and communicate with facility with any particular point that might be pressed. I will trouble you at your next visit to consider how far such a thing would be desirable, and whether the ground will conveniently admit of it, and, further, if the same sort of course could be introduced to advantage between the southern of the three mill redoubts (on the right) and the Tagus.

Celorico, 19*th August*, 1810.

SIR,

I THIS morning received your letter of the 14th, and have to acquaint you, that the Commander of the Forces approves of the allowance of a dollar per diem being granted to Lieut. Jeronimo José Ferreira and Captain Manoel Marquis de Cintra, as proposed by you.

I am, Sir.

Alverca da Beira, 24*th August*, 1810.

MY DEAR SIR,

I HAVE been favoured with your letter of the 17th, on the subject of the ground commanding the new redoubt above Oeyras. I cannot express how much I feel obliged by all your suggestions to promote the service. I would wish, however, before I speak to Lord Wellington on the immediate subject of your last letter, to be enabled to answer any questions he might put to me, as far as circumstances may admit.

Perhaps you will be able to give me some rough idea of the quantity of powder that might be required for the operation you propose.

With respect to the ground on the left of the Alhandra position, I have often been uneasy in considering it. I was anxious, whilst our time seemed very limited, not to propose more works than there seemed to be an immediate probability of executing, and I have lately been much occupied in thinking at what point fortifications ought to stop, should we remain here through the winter. The redoubt near Trancosa was thrown up under a hope that it might prevent an enemy from turning the position of Alhandra with artillery—infantry would, I believe, undoubtedly do it. If, on a minute examination of the ground, you think that 1500 men might be so entrenched as to prevent the last mentioned species of force from penetrating; the object, is, I conceive, highly important, and I shall be truly obliged by your ideas at large on this matter.

I would not draw any of the tools from the places at which they are now in use to form the depôt at Coimbra.

Alverca da Beira, *27th August*, 1810.

My dear Sir,

I received your letter of the 22d instant, on the subject of our works near St. Julian's, yesterday morning.

I am glad to find the ground between the redoubts on the left of the position favourable for forming covered communications between them.

With respect to the interval between the cliff and the most southern of the mill redoubts, I had thought that some sort of line there would have a much better command of the ground in front than a work situated at the stone quarry in the rear, which would see but a short distance before it, and would itself be much better commanded by guns, or even musketry, that would be shouldered against the fire of the mill redoubts, by the shape of the ground.

I dare say, however, you will be able to manage the defilement of the work, so as to correct the evil of command, and I wish to abide entirely by what you think best on the spot. I think my general authority from Lord Wellington on this head sufficient for the execution of either. For the sake of despatch, I think I would not have the capacity of the works exceed what would be necessary for about 300 men. The guns you can best decide. I am glad to find you have actually set about shaping the hill opposed to our last-erected work, so that it may be rendered of little service to an enemy.

I am, &c.

(Extract.)

Celorico, 29*th August,* 1810.

ALMEIDA is taken, owing, it is said, to their principal magazine having exploded. . . . . . It is impossible to see very far at present, but as things are, I am anxious to have whatever you think best done at St. Julian's, (the place of embarkation,) as soon as possible.

(Confidential.)

Celorico, 31*st August,* 1810.

MY DEAR SIR,

I HAVE this moment been with Lord Wellington, to ask him to what extent he would have our position put into an immediate state of defence. Whether the abattis should be felled, embankments on the Tagus levelled, &c. His Lordship says, that the former he would have undertaken directly, the latter he would not begin to throw down as yet. You will recollect there is one running along the river in front of redoubt No. 33, on the right of the position of the Serra de Serves, and another in front of that work; these it was intended ultimately to remove. There are a great many olive trees between No. 39 and the road, which were intended to be felled into separate rows of abattis. You will find, I think, many parts of the line between Morugeira, (in the pass of Mafra and Ribamar,) in which trees may be felled to advantage. The same thing will, I think, also apply in other situations. I need not say, that all the roads intended to be mined should be in a perfect state of readiness. Is the bridge in rear of Bucellas mined? I do not know that its destruction would do much good; but we have mined bridges in this neighbourhood that will not perhaps do more. There is an arch across a gulley between Alverca and our works on the right of the Serra da Serves—does it seem worth while to mine this? There is a bridge in the rear of Enaxara dos Cavallerios which might be considered. Lord Wellington wishes the ammunition to be put into the different works as soon as possible. I would have you complete the communication between the redoubts on the left of the St. Julian's position as soon as you can. You will, I am sure, do your best on the right of this position. I am quite satisfied that you will quickly do what is most advantageous on the whole, with the time and means in your power. Are all the redoubts numbered?

Your's very truly.

Celorico, *2d September*, 1810.

SIR,

I AM this morning favoured with your letter of the 29th ultimo, relative to the position of Alhandra, your report on its present state, and your proposals to prevent its being turned. I immediately submitted the whole to Lord Wellington for his consideration. He thinks, that, on the whole, it is desirable to strengthen the ground on the immediate left of the valley, and he would have you begin without loss of time.

I think I would, in the first instance, begin the lower work in front, unless, if being unsupported, it would be too liable to be carried by musketry. As to the others, I would recommend your immediately providing a depôt of palisades, that should the occasion press, you may be in some state of defence against assault. In short, to progressively strengthen the ground in whatever way you think best.

Gouvea, *7th September*, 1810.

Lord Wellington has just now told me, that the artillery officer ordered to inspect the state of the ammunition has reported, that the numbers of our different works are not correct.

If from any cause the works are not all marked by their numbers on a board, you will oblige me by having it done as soon as possible. I before wrote to you as to distinguishing the works undertaken since I quitted Lisbon by letters. Do you think it would be worth while to mark any of the new flanking points taken up on the position of Alhandra? Since I wrote the above I have seen Lord Wellington, and he prefers numbers for the new works, though they may not be in regular succession; I would, therefore, propose that you mark the left of the new works behind the Zizandra 110, and go on regularly with the numbers to the right of Alhandra.

As it is the intention of the Admiral to withdraw the navy from our signal posts, Lord Wellington requests you will make an arrangement that the ordinanças may take charge of them for the present. You can use his name as your authority for any step you may take in that way. Do you think it would be practicable to find a set of men whom one could trust to work them, or who could be made to understand them?

R. F.

P. S.—Lord Wellington says, at all events cut the trenches through the salt pans.

(Extract.)

Gouvea, *9th September*, 1810.

I WISH I may not in my zeal have got into a scrape about the water casks. Lord Wellington seems to think the undertaking too great, and desires to have a list of the numbers that will be required. Can you therefore stop your hand for the present? Should they still be allowed, could not the commissary-general supply a part of them?

Gouvea, *11th September*, 1810.

IN consequence of the Admiral having decided to withdraw the navy from our signal posts, Lord Wellington thinks we had better use the simple Portugueze telegraph, and I request you will have the goodness to get one made for each post and carried to the spot. I should think it will not be difficult for you to procure a sufficient number of old seamen at Lisbon to work them.

Lord Wellington has consented that the water casks should be supplied, and will order the commissary-general to furnish and pay for them.

Cortiça, *20th September*, 1810.

Lord Wellington requests you will inform Mr. Dunmore that you think you can press the water casks. He will write to Col. Peacocke relative to the captain and two privates for each signal post.

Coimbra, *30th September*, 1810.

Sir,

I have to acknowledge the receipt of your letter of the 22d instant, recommending that a redoubt should be thrown up for 300 men, somewhere about the centre of the line extending from the heights of Calhandrix to the Serra de Serves, and that the latter should be scarped where necessary.

His Lordship, the Commander of the Forces, is pleased to approve these proposals, and to direct that they shall be carried into effect as soon as possible.

(Confidential, enclosed in the above, same date.)

Dear Sir,

Present circumstances seem to render it necessary that every precaution should be taken at and near our works for their being immediately occupied and defended, should such a measure become expedient. I would therefore recommend your making every arrangement as to mining roads, felling abattis, clearing away obstacles, dressing off slopes, &c. &c., with the various other necessary precautions, not any of which I well know will escape your observation. I would not actually load the mines until the last extremity.

Head Quarters, Leiria, *2d October,* 1810.

My dear Sir,

The following services have occurred to me as being necessary, under present circumstances, to be performed immediately: viz. making the distributions of the hand-grenades to the different works; getting the water casks into them; making a banquette to the walls which defend the left of the valley in front of Via Longa; making a good trench for musketry across this valley, I should think in the road leading to the height on the right, or rather on one side of this road where there is now a bank with some aloes, connecting by some kind of musketry defence with the village of Boca de Lapa. As there must be a number of guns placed on the high point on the right of this valley, I think it might be desirable to throw up a redoubt on this spot, having six embrasures towards the low ground. I think there should also be an emplacement for guns at the mill at the end of the wall on the left, and to stockade or enclose it. In general, whatever you can do with the time and means in your power for defence at this ground, I think should be undertaken. The line-wall on the Tagus in front of the right of No. 33 to be levelled. The line immediately parallel to its front to be levelled. The bridge at Torres Vedras on the road to Sobral to be mined, in case it should become advisable to destroy it, and if any impediment would be occasioned by its destruction. These are all the additions that occur to me at present. Should you observe that I have omitted any thing in my several letters, I beg you will have the goodness to do whatever you think necessary towards the defence of our positions. Lord Wellington will write to the Admiral relative to gun-boats for our right flank. Are our new telegraphs completed?

Your's, &c.

Alcobaça, *5th October*, 1810.

Dear Sir,

Lord Wellington has directed me to write to you on the subject of guides for the different districts of our works. His Lordship has divided the districts as follows:—

No. 1. From the sea to Torres Vedras; head-quarters, Torres Vedras.

No. 2. From Sobral de Monte Agraça to the valley of Calhandrix; head-quarters, Sobral de Monte Agraça.

No. 3. From the valley of Calhandrix to the Tagus on the right of Alhandra; head-quarters, Alhandra.

No. 4. From the banks of the Tagus near Alverca to the pass of Bucellas inclusive; head-quarters, Bucellas.

No. 5. From the pass of Freixal inclusive to the right of the pass of Mafra, including Enaxarados Cavalleiros; head-quarters, Montachique.

No. 6. From the pass of Mafra inclusive to the sea; head-quarters, Mafra.

Lord Wellington wishes that an officer of the ordinanças, or any other respectable person well qualified from local knowledge, should be appointed, with about four men under him, also well qualified, to show the roads from the works along the positions, and those leading to them from the front, connecting with the next district by the flanks, and to the rear, in case of necessity. The officers and a part of the men must be mounted, and a letter will be written to Mr. Dunmore to supply good mules for them; let us say for the officers and two of the men for each district, if possible. I am sure you will make every arrangement for this service immediately. Lord Wellington wishes that the officer of each district should be in readiness to meet the quarter-master-general when we retire, and that the men should all be on the spot.

I would recommend that the men should be constantly practised in acquiring every information about the roads of and bordering on the several districts. Every possible preparation is now of course necessary towards the defence of our works.

The officers of guides will have cavalry pay, and the men 1*s*. 6*d*. per diem.

I am very anxious about our signal posts.

I am, dear Sir.

Head-Quarters, Rio-mayor, *6th October*, 1810.

My dear Sir,

I have named the officers to the several districts as follows:—

No. 1. Captain Mulcaster, Lieut. Thomson.
2. Captain Goldfinch, Lieut. Forster.
3. Captain Squire, Lieut. Piper.
4. Captain Burgoyne, Lieut. Stanway.
5. Captain Dickinson, Lieut. Trench.
6. Captain Ross, Lieut. Hulme.

I have not named you for a district, as I think you will be much more useful to act generally in the first instance. I will trouble you to order all the above officers with you to join at the head-quarters of the different districts as soon as possible.

Lord Wellington says he will not part with the seamen now, if they are not gone. I think you had better meet us as soon as you can. I believe head-quarters will be at Sobral on the 9th, where I shall be happy to meet you.

Aruda, *10th October*, 1810.

My dear Sir,

I am very anxious to have the pleasure of seeing you. Can you come to head-quarters this evening? we will take the best care we can of you. Would it not be well to take Lieut. Reid's men from the redoubt he is now throwing up and send them to those in front of Cabo. I am not quite easy about that village; you will oblige me by giving directions to put all the strength possible towards strengthening it, in any way as far as trenches, banquetting, walls, and any thing else that may occur to you can be done.

R. Fletcher.

Captain Jones, R. E.

LETTERS AND REPORTS

FROM

CAPTAIN J. T. JONES

TO

LIEUTENANT COLONEL FLETCHER.

Lisbon, 18*th July*, 1810.

I AM sorry I cannot give you a favourable account of the signal stations; the sailors say, that the distance between the stations is too great, and that the masts are all too light for the yards; on Sunday evening two were sprung: they also complain of the telescopes. I have ordered stronger masts and yards to be prepared for each post, and if better telescopes can be procured in Lisbon, I shall not hesitate to authorise the purchase of them. To render the Ponte de Rol signals visible we are cutting down the pine-wood, which at present forms its back-ground.

The new works, Nos. 88. 90 and 91, are pushing forward with the utmost exertion by

Lieut. Hulme; the guns for them are on the spot.

Alhandra, 25*th July*, 1810.

SIR,

I HAVE the honour to report, that, in obedience to your orders of the 17th from Alverca de Beira, the front of this position has been carefully examined, and such parts of it have been marked for scarping as appear eligible; and various flanks and redoubts have been traced out in situations favourable for sweeping the face of the hill. A body of peasantry has been demanded of the government and will commence these operations to-morrow, and I feel I may venture to assure you, that with six weeks or two months' labour, the whole of the front of the position shall be made as strong as can reasonably be desired.

(*Extracts.*)

Via Longa, 3*d August*, 1810.

YOUR letter of the 31st from Celorico has been a great relief to me, as I think it ensures us the time necessary to complete the works begun since your departure, except, of course, the position of Alhandra, and even that will be in a forward state. The new work at Oeyras will be very shortly in a fair state of defence. No. 88. 90 and 91, are already in such a forward state, that I yesterday took all the workmen, (except 50 each,) and sent them to St. Pedro to push on those works. I have directed Capt. Williams to confine his exertions at Monte Agraça solely to making the work defensible, such as clearing out the ditches, filling up the openings through the counterscarps, &c.

The rains last week did much damage to the works and we have parties everywhere employed to put them into order.

(Extract.)

I passed a message from Alhandra to Mafra by our chain of posts in —— minutes, so that there is now no fear of their answering when the weather is tolerably clear.

How far might it be expedient to provide water casks, with three days' water for the garrison of each redoubt? The men may bring with them three days' provisions, but they cannot bring three days' water, and it is scarcely possible to exist for six hours under fatigue in summer without liquid. A redoubt may not be attacked, and still for many days no man dare go half a league distant in search of water, and there is none nearer to some of the works.

Water tubs for the batteries are in preparation.

(Private.)

5th August, 1810.

PRAY have the kindness to ask Lord Wellington to write to Don Miguel Forjas on the subject of furnishing us every man the country can supply; it would incline the Portugueze government to pay more attention to our representations generally. I have complained to Don Miguel and to Don Antonio Souares de Noronha, the captain-general of the province, on this subject, and they have severely reprehended the several capitaōs-mor, particularly those I had reported by name; but they every one protest, that all the ordinanzas of a middle age have been taken from them for the militia, and that none are left but boys and old men.

9th August.

I HAVE sent an order to Capt. Williams to join general Leith's corps without the smallest delay, and have ordered Lieut. Trench to take charge and complete the Sobral works.

I regret exceedingly not being able to get forward with a general plan of the lines; but by the subjoined distribution of the officers you will see it is impossible, at present, to withdraw any one from his particular duty.

Captain	Holloway, . .	Peniche.
	Wedekind, . .	Sick.
	Dickinson, . .	Setuval.
Lieut.	Meinecke, . .	Oeyras.
	Forster, . . .	Alhandra.
	Trench, . . .	Sobral.
	Piper, . . .	Alhandra.
	Tapp, . . .	Lisbon Duty.
	Reid, ...	St. Pedro de Cadeira.
	Hulme, . . .	Mafra and Ericeira.

In all of which districts there are very considerable working parties employed; but I hope after next week to make some arrangement for the plan.

Mafra, 14*th August*, 1810.

Sir,

I visited Setuval on the 7th of this month, and in consequence of the then state of affairs, as communicated in your letter of the 29th ult., I abridged considerably the work which had been planned there. I likewise exerted myself to the utmost, and with some success, to procure more workmen and enforce more attention from the officers of ordinanzas; notwithstanding which I do not think those works will be completed before the middle of the ensuing month. Capt. Dickinson seems to think a fortnight more will suffice for their completion, and I send you an extract from his last report to me on the subject.

(Extract.)

Setuval, *9th August*, 1810.

The last orders received by the governor here had so good an effect, that he informed me yesterday, on his return from Lisbon, that six hundred workmen would be furnished me next week, attended by officers of ordinanzas and by a guard of twenty soldiers, for the purpose of taking all unruly subjects into custody: they will be distributed between the large redoubt, the lines, the two small redoubts in front, and the old pentagon. I am in immediate want of two barrels of gunpowder, for nothing but rock presents itself where I am excavating. I am in great hopes of having all completed here in a fortnight.

S. Dickinson.

Captain Jones,
Comm. Engineer.

18th August, 1810.

Sir,

On the subject of the Figueiras regiment of militia, again mentioned in your letter of the 12th, I beg to say, that I am no longer desirous of retaining them, having failed in my best endeavours to move them from Mafra, in which district we now procure peasantry sufficient for the work.

On the 1st August I wrote to Don Miguel Forjas, the Secretary at War, requesting he would issue orders for their march from Mafra to Alhandra, to be employed on the new defences. On the 4th Don Miguel replied, that the regiment having been stationed at Mafra by order of Marshal Beresford, it was necessary to have the Marshal's order for their removal. I wrote to Marshal Beresford's headquarters that same day, to request their removal to Alhandra, but have not yet had any reply.

Immediately upon the receipt of your letter yesterday I wrote to the commanding officer of the regiment to say, that his men are no longer required for service of the works, and that, as far as the engineer department is concerned, he is at full liberty to dispose of his men as he may think proper. I conceive, however, that some further order to the colonel will be necessary for their removal.

(Private.)

August, 1810.

Of Alhandra I hope we shall form a very strong position. I consider it now a strong position for 10,000 men, a fortnight hence I hope it will be thought the same for 7,000 men, and in a month I doubt whether more than 5,000 will be required for its defence.

Alhandra, however, does not altogether satisfy me as a position; I should fear that an enemy acting with a very superior force would penetrate by the hills on the left and get possession of the serra in the rear of it—a movement which would not only turn all our defences, but might perhaps lead to the capture of the whole force in the position, as it would then find itself surrounded and its retreat cut off.

On riding over the ground above A dos Matos, it appeared to me, that a post for 1500 men might be established there, which would effectually prevent such an enterprise. I feel diffident, however, in making the proposal; but, although no advocate for multiplying works, the necessity for creating some obstruction to the march of an enemy along the heights on the other side of the valley which bounds the left of the Alhandra position, is so thoroughly impressed on my mind, that I believe I shall suppress all other feelings and write to you officially on the subject; perhaps a strong work for a battalion on the rear serra itself might answer every end. When the mind is deeply engaged on any object, various thoughts and ideas occur which appear reasonable to the person forming them, and yet are in themselves absurd and will not bear investigation. Such, perhaps, is my case now, but I cannot avoid thinking that Alhandra should not be left an isolated position, but be joined to the Ajuda works, and that 2000 men strongly entrenched on its left would serve to connect the country into one defensive line from the Tagus to the Ajuda valley.

Lisbon, 29*th August*, 1810.

SIR,

IN consequence of your wishes I have now the honour to enter into some detail respecting the position at Alhandra and of the means to prevent its being turned. I enclose a paper of memoranda which I drew up yesterday when on the spot—it must be read as relating to the state of the work on Saturday next, and will I hope prove a satisfactory account of that strong position.

The ground on the opposite side of the valley on the left is a range of strong hills of a much superior elevation to any other ground near them, and connected by a regular descent with the hills in rear of the position.

At a point about a mile retired from the front of the Alhandra position this ridge terminates to its left with a bluff point, which overlooks all the country to the Ajuda works, at the distance perhaps in a straight line between them of less than three miles; at this spot it appears to me that a post might be formed for 1500 men, extending completely across the ridge, one flank of which shall appui on the bluff point, and consequently overlook the country in that direction, and the other flank rest on the valley which forms the left of the Alhandra position, and its fire co-operate with the Alhandra redoubts in preventing the passage of an enemy through the valley.

This post would so thoroughly occupy these hills as to prevent the march of infantry to the rear otherwise than by the space of two or three miles between it and the Ajuda works, and it would leave the whole army at liberty to act in that difficult country, whilst the enemy would have the garrisons of Sobral and Alhandra in their rear, and I should conceive it too hazardous an enterprise for them to attempt —if that be admitted, it follows, that it would secure Alhandra from being turned by an enemy with or without artillery. I have one feeling of doubt on my mind, which it is my duty to state, and that is, the possibility of an enemy forcing the valley between the two works. I will here state what has been done to secure it, and if not judged sufficient, orders may be sent for further obstacles being created: at its entrance, eight 12-pounders, in inattackable situations, can shower down grape shot upon the enemy, and during a passage of half a mile they will always be under the fire of at least six pieces of that nature of ordnance, and for some part of the way under ten; the work now proposed will give an additional cross fire, and will prevent an entry into the valley by a collateral branch which exists about midway, and which is a most serious disadvantage: it is, however, to be recollected, that the fire of the artillery is from a very great height, and that much cover is created in the valley by hollow ways and steep rising grounds, and that in the night the fire of artillery will of course be uncertain; when an attack is expected, it will be proper to cut down the trees and place them as an additional obstacle across the valley, and also to level the houses, walls, &c. The works I propose to construct are three redoubts for 400 men each, mutually flanking each other, with a smaller work in advance to look down the valley in front, which the three forming the position cannot do: it is proposed to make them to resist cannon, and they being nearly a mile retired from the front of the Alhandra position, I do not think any enemy dare to bring up artillery for their reduction without having first forced Alhandra, for as the rear of that post will be open to our army and hid from him, he can never tell whether there be 4000 or 14,000 men in it.

I have sent a hasty sketch from memory of the ground, but which I trust will be sufficient to point out the situation of the proposed works, The soil is very unfavourable for their construction, it will therefore require nearly two months to complete them from the day of their commencement.

(Memoranda referred to in the foregoing Letter.)

The position of Alhandra, as now taken up, is formed of an isolated range of heights; its right bounded by the Tagus, its front, left, and part of the rear by a deep and difficult valley.

It may be viewed under the divisions of its front, left flank, and rear.

The front naturally subdivides into two parts: 1st. An extent of upwards of 2000 yards on the left, which has been so cut and blasted along its summit, as to give it a continued scarp every where exceeding 10 feet in height, flanked in its whole length by musketry and cannon, and the approach to the scarp lying under a fire of grape shot: large general flanks have been established for that purpose, and redoubts have been erected on the summit for the security of the guns and troops should any part of the position be forced. The second division of the front is an extent of 700 yards, more than half of it the low flat ground bounding the Tagus; the remainder is the slope of a hill of easy ascent, gradually rising from the low ground till it meets the artificial scarp. This whole length has been retrenched by a continued flanked line of a strong profile; across the low ground an advanced ditch has been added, flanked from the line ascending the hill, and which has likewise been made to answer as a powerful flank to the low ground generally. At the left extremity of this line, and at the point where the nearly inaccessible part of the front ceases, a redoubt has been thrown up.

The left of the position may be considered as having a front of half a mile. The ground is very high and steep, but not inaccessible. Two redoubts have been established there, the one on the most commanding point of the whole position, for 400 men and eight 12-pounders, the other on the left, for 350 men and six 12-pounders. A species of redoubt or flèche has been thrown up where the nearly inaccessible part of the front finishes on the left, for which perhaps 150 men should be apportioned, as in case of necessity they can support the front or flank as either may be pressed. Scarping and other impediments of that nature have also been attempted with success, so that the left flank may be considered only less strong than the front.

The rear of the position is above two and a half miles in extent. It is very open and of easy ascent, and one part of it is commanded by a range of hills, the occupation of which by an enemy would turn all our defences, and most probably cut off the retreat of the troops.

There are but three ways by which an enemy can get in the rear, or obtain possession of the above mentioned ridge of hills. 1st. By forcing his way through the valley on the left. 2d. By marching a column along the opposite heights of Calhandrix parallel to the left flank. 3d. By making a detour to his right of several miles. To guard against the first, a height detached in advance of the position on the left has been occupied by a work for 250 men and five 12-pounders, and which, from its situation and construction, is so strong, that it ought never to be forced: the fire from this work and from the redoubts, with an abattis, may, perhaps, be deemed sufficient to prevent an enemy from passing along the valley. The second passage might be impeded by the construction of a post for 1500 men upon the hills parallel to the left flank: at present to carry artillery by that route, it would be only requisite for the enemy to force the redoubt above Trancoso. The third method can only be properly opposed by the manœuvres of the general commanding the army; but its bad effects might probably be counteracted by the erection of a strong work on the rear range of hills, where it would be the object of an enemy to establish himself.

J. T. J.

The above Reports on Alhandra are printed in full, with the view of giving some insight into the details of the labours of 1810.

Lisbon, *3d Sept.* 1810.

This morning I marked out a line to the right of the mill redoubts at Oeyras (agreeably with your letter of the 27th ult.) and which I hope in ten days time to render an obstacle to an enemy attempting to penetrate by that flank.

Your confidential letter of the 31st has just been received. I am happy to have it in my power to say that every thing at Oeyras is in a proper state, and I trust whenever the army falls back every thing will be found as it ought to be.

Lisbon, *5th Sept.* 1810.

Dear Sir,

Your letters of the 1st and 2d instant have been this day received. We will to-morrow commence strengthening the ground to the left of Alhandra. I cannot say from recollection whether the narrow part in front of the proposed redoubts can be cut through, but I think, with plenty of time, much might be done by scarping. You may depend upon every exertion being used to do the utmost our means will allow at that spot. As you did not before notice my suggestion for water-casks being provided for the different redoubts, I concluded it had not been approved of. I have this morning set about endeavouring to collect casks sufficient to hold 10,000 gallons of water: water-tubs I have been collecting for some time past.

With respect to the salt-pans on the right of Via Longa, we have made a cut through the low ground, or rather, we have widened and deepened a ditch which already existed there. We did it as a substitute for the cut ordered by you, in consequence of the opposition our proceedings met with, and from the damage which they would occasion to private property. I mentioned in a former letter that the Marchioness of Abrantes, who derives a great revenue from the salt works, had made a representation to our minister to stop the work, and that Mr. Stuart had written to me on the subject. I should, however, much like authority to proceed again with the original cut, as it is in every way better than its substitute; at all events, the salt-pans shall be filled the moment it appears necessary. Lieutenant Stanway is forming the abattis at that position. We are likewise mining the bridge at Bucellas and near Enaxara—of course it is all done as quietly as possible. As to the magazines being damp, as far as my observation goes I have never seen any of the same nature less so: they have all been lined with boards since your departure and every other precaution has been taken to keep them dry: whoever made the statement can have had but very little experience of the nature of field magazines, or must have made the observation from a wish to find fault; that the magazines will be damp when the rains set in, is beyond a doubt, but that they are damp now, I deny. The platforms of every work have been relaid since your departure. The work on the right of Freixal is raising, but with very little advantage or effect. We are going on with the line on the right of the mill redoubts at Oeyras, and I hope to make it something respectable in ten days' time; the ground is extremely rocky and otherwise unfavourable for excavating. As to the trench to join the redoubts, we have not workmen sufficient to undertake it in toto. We will put them upon it as far as they will extend, and the remainder of the trench being marked out, in case of emergency, a couple of thousand soldiers can complete it in twenty-four hours. For these operations we have been obliged to withdraw 100 men from sloping the hill.

(Extract.)

Lisbon, 8th Sept. 1810.

On the subject of a general system of drainage for the works before the rains set in, I conceive it to be absolutely necessary for their preservation during the winter—we have had a few showers lately, the effects of which have been to bring down the fascine work and to deface the slopes, and, in some parts, to bring down the scarps. Parties have been constantly employed repairing these damages. I will take the earliest opportunity to examine the different works with this view, and to give more plunge to the superior slopes which may require it. Lieut. Hulme having made great progress with the several mines which we consider necessary under the roads and bridges on the left, I have ordered him for this duty, and for improving the defence of Freixal, and we were to have started together this morning, but the subjoined letter from Lieut. Reid renders it necessary that I should go to Mafra to see to the abattis at Morgueira and to perfecting the defences of the valley on its left.

St. Pedro de Cadera, *6th Sept.* 1810.

DEAR SIR,

AFTER I sent off my letter to you last night I received a letter from Lieutenant Hulme to say that he had received your orders, through Lieutenant Stanway, to show me the mines and every thing to be done in that district, and then that he was to go immediately to Lisbon, I therefore went over the Ereceira works with him to day. You had desired him to form an abattis from Morgueira to Ribamar: this I shall begin immediately, though I must say I have not all the confidence I could wish. If you have time, I would be much obliged to you for some further instructions; however, as I conceive that there is no time at present for delay, I shall go over the Morgueira ground to-morrow, and the instant I can collect cars and men I shall begin at that place and form a connected line from one redoubt to the other, breaking it in such places as will give me the most advantageous flank in front of my trees. I shall most anxiously look out for a note from you to say if this is what you wish.

I remain, &c.

WILLIAM REID, Lieut. R. E.

Capt. JONES,
Comm. Eng.

P. S.—The two redoubts of Lieut. Thomson, near this, I expect are this night completed with plank platform.

11th Sept. 1810.—*Evening.*

REDOUBTS 88. 90 and 91, on the Picanceira line, are completely finished, and we are doing our utmost to strengthen the face of the ravine by scarping and laying it open to the fire of the work.

With respect to Oeyras, as I could not visit it this week from being so much occupied with the Mongueira abattis, the Picanceira line, and the various new works on the right, I beg to enclose a report I have this instant received from Captain Wedekind.

Oeyras, *11th Sept.* 1810.

SIR,

I SHOULD have reported to you before this on the progress of the new lines lately began had I not been in the hopes of your weekly inspection of this district. With the means I have at present I calculate to have the flèche near the sea side in some state of defence by the end of next week or the 21st of this month, that is, the ditch 15 feet wide at top and 9 feet deep, and the parapet 7 feet 6 inches high and 10 feet thick at top, and the lines between it and the mill redoubts, the ditches 12 feet wide and 4 feet deep.

The soil where the flèche is is as bad as possible, that of the lines is more favourable: the ditches are opened at a distance of 170 yards, 6 feet deep and 4 feet high parapet; there are about 400 more yards of ditch to be opened.

No. 109 redoubt is palisaded and shall leave there to-morrow only 100 men to improve the glacis and counterscarp on the west side: the masons are about laying the three last platforms of stone: the magazine is complete.

I propose to begin the opening of the trench between 106 and 107 on Monday, if you can send me the 500 tools specified in the accompanying requisition: the distance between these works is nearly 800 yards.

I shall be much obliged if you will have the goodness to hasten at the commissary-general's the delivery of the remaining palisades, since my last demand approved by you on the 10th August, to complete which near 3000 are as yet wanting.

I shall continue my utmost exertions to make the best of the means I have to forward the works.

CHARLES WEDEKIND,
Capt. Eng. K.G.L.

Captain JONES,
Comm. Engineer.

Lisbon, 12th Sept. 1810.

DEAR SIR,

I HAVE stopped collecting the water-casks; none had been absolutely purchased—only bespoke. Whenever occasion requires it, I can, at two days' notice, seize casks enough in the cellars of the vineyards around to supply all the works with water, and I think such would be the most eligible plan.

I do not believe that any of the redoubts have wrong numbers affixed to them; at least, we carry on our duty by numbers and not by names, and I have never yet found any mistake to arise. I will, however, have them all examined.

Taking away the seamen from the signal posts will be a misfortune, as they have just become thoroughly expert at passing the signals. I think that a non-commissioned officer and two privates might be selected from Lisbon for each post, whom we could trust to pass the signals; but I do not think we could ever teach Portugueze, and even with soldiers I am not very sanguine in my expectations of rendering them very expert.

The abattis near Via Longa are very forward, and to-morrow the cut through the salt-pans shall be recommenced.

I have not yet been able to discover one magazine in the slightest degree damp.

Lisbon, *18th September*, 1810.

I HAVE applied for and am promised Portugueze guards for all the signal stations, and as soon as it is reported to me that they have mounted, I will write to the Admiral according to your directions.

Artificers are employed constructing the portable telegraphs to be fixed up near the site of the present signal staffs. The post was removed from the Picanceira redoubt to Marvoa, and now answers very well.

(Private.)

I AM happy to say the arrangement I made with Don Miguel Forjas, that the governors of

Mafra and Sacavem shall receive our orders for men for the right and left respectively, and see that the several capitaõs-mor furnish their full contingents, has done wonders for us. I expect we shall have 2,000 additional this week, including women and boys, whom I pay at one-half and one-fourth the price of men. At Alhandra our numbers are so great that Forster has been obliged to turn commissary and procure bread and serve it out as rations, in order to enable them to subsist.

22d Sept.

Sir,

Not feeling myself authorised to sanction the appointment which Captain Holloway reports to me on the other side to have made at Peniche, I have written to him to say so, and that I shall forward his letter to you for a decision thereupon, which I now do.

(Signed) J. T. J.

The side arms, &c. are all complete, with the guns, &c. in all the new flanks and new works; indeed, General Rosa and his Portugueze artillerymen have shown the greatest zeal and activity in complying with our demands.

5th October, 1810.

I ORDERD the hand-grenades to be put into the magazines at the same time with the ammunition, and the water casks into the several works.

Three of the new telegraphs were not quite complete last evening, but I expect in the course of to-morrow to fix those for the advanced line of signals in their places.

I begun the new redoubt between Alhandra and the Serra de Serves on the 3d, the day I received the authority, and yesterday we began in earnest to scarp the Serra de Serves. From this moment every thing shall give way to the position of Via Longa.

I trust you will find every thing to your wishes. I spare no exertion to have all the works, &c. in the most creditable order, and I find the utmost attention and exertion in all the officers.

Alhandra, *6th October*, 1810.

I DULY received your letter from Leiria, and I can now venture to assure you, that every preparation for an instant defence of the lines is complete, and you need be under no apprehension for our credit, even if the enemy attack as the rear division enters the works.

The moment I knew of the army having commenced its retrograde movements, I commenced our final preparations; and we have neither spared houses, gardens, vineyards, olive trees, woods, or private property of any description: the only blind to the fire of the works now standing is that beautiful avenue of old trees in the pass of Torres Vedras. The Juez da Fora and inhabitants pleaded to me so hard for the latest moment, lest they might be unnecessarily cut down, that I have consented to defer it till the day before the troops march in, and as I have trust-worthy men with axes in readiness on the spot, there is no doubt of their being felled in time. The pine woods on the Torres heights are down and formed into abattis.

The abattis at Via Longa is also complete, the openings for communications being stopped up; the cut and salt pans are full of water, and Lieut. Stanway will finish levelling the banks, &c. to-night. The water casks and hand-grenades are furnished to every redoubt. The powder is in the cases to load the mines, and the officers, each in his own district, is prepared to meet the divisions. The telegraphs for the front line of posts were forwarded from Lisbon yesterday.

It is lucky we commenced dressing off so

soon, for now every thing is in confusion: the people are all running away; and a string of men, women, and children, in cars, on animals, and on foot, are crowding every road to Lisbon. No one will believe that the army will halt till it reaches St. Julian's, and all authority and order is beginning to be lost. Besides, the fore-runners of the army seize every thing, and

. . . .

I flatter myself you will be altogether surprised at the formidable appearance of our scarps here, and much pleased with the quantity of work of every nature done since your departure. When I heard of the Busaco business, I began to be alarmed for the consequences of having done so much; for if the lines had not come into play, the expense would most likely have been cavilled at as unnecessary; but now of course only the benefit derived from the strength of the works will be considered.

(Signed) JOHN T. JONES.

LIEUT. COL. FLETCHER.

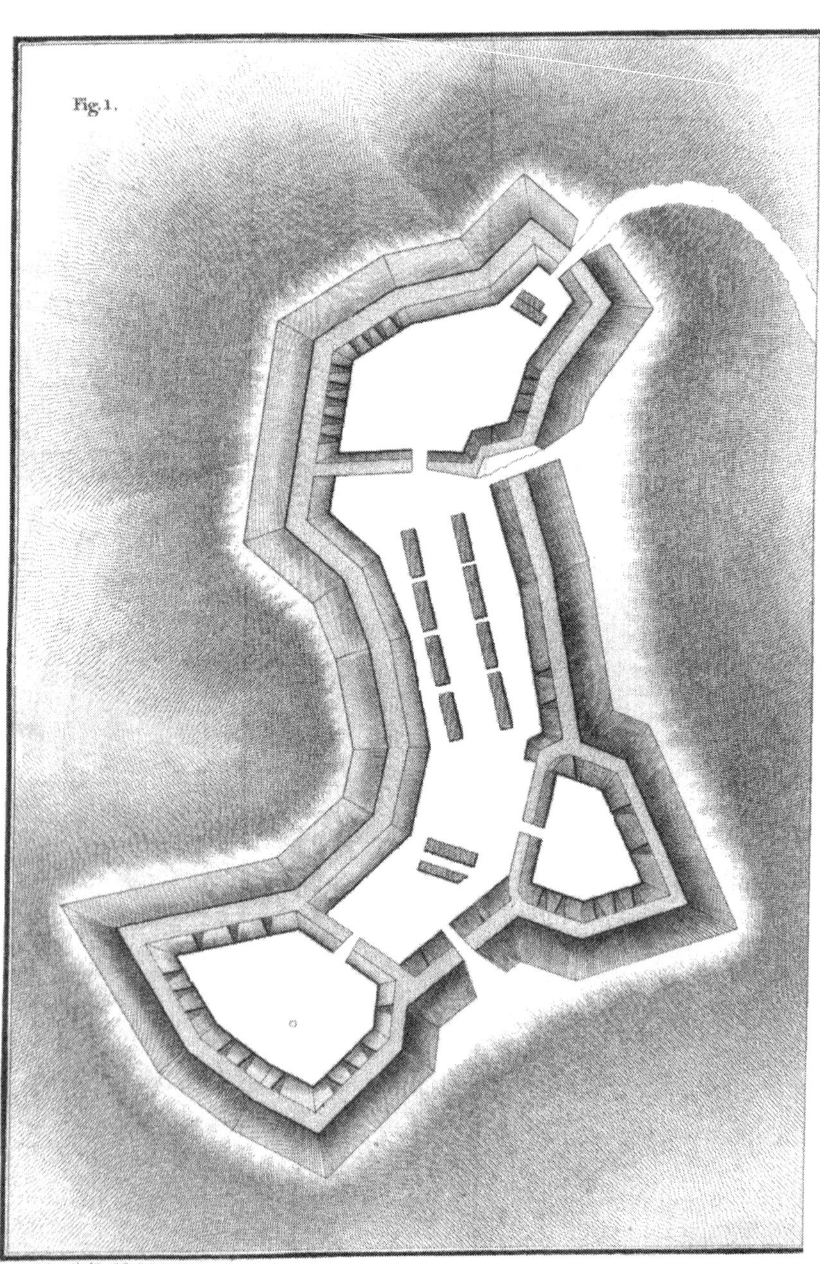
Fig. 1.

Plate 1.

Fig. 2.

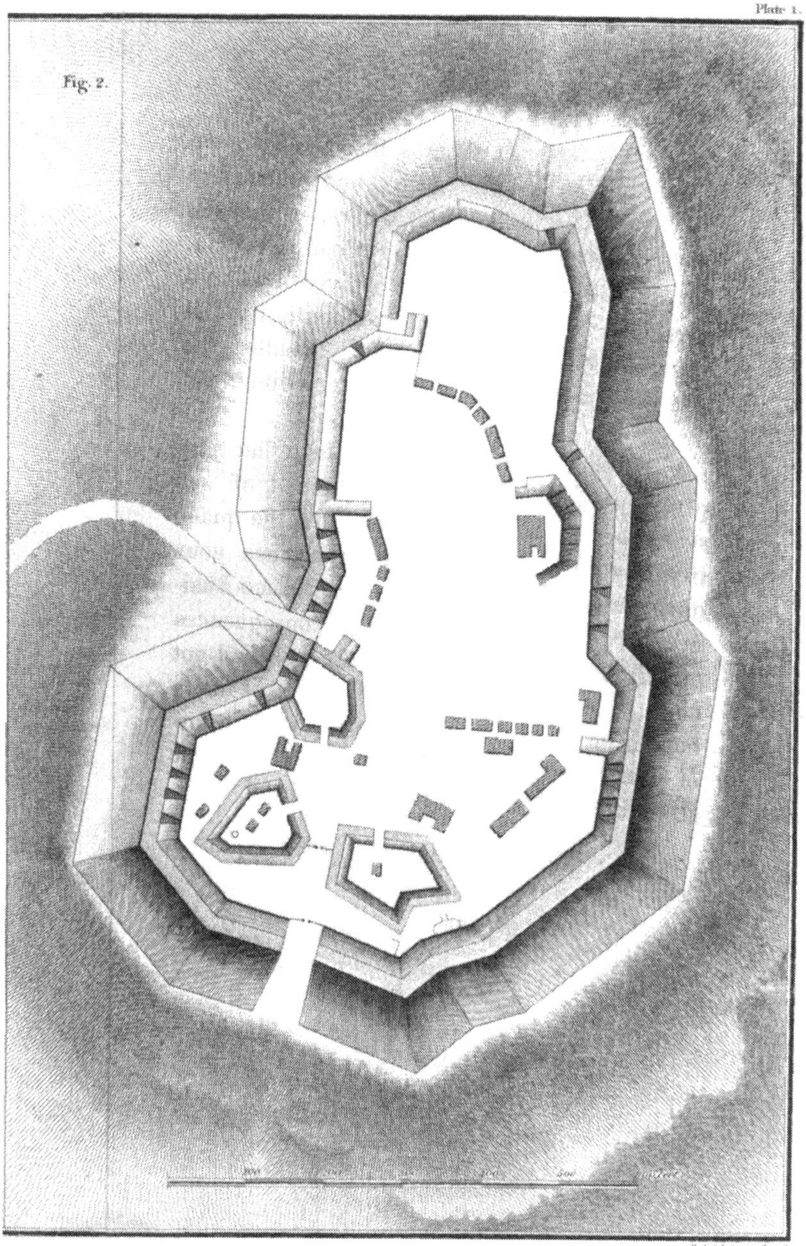

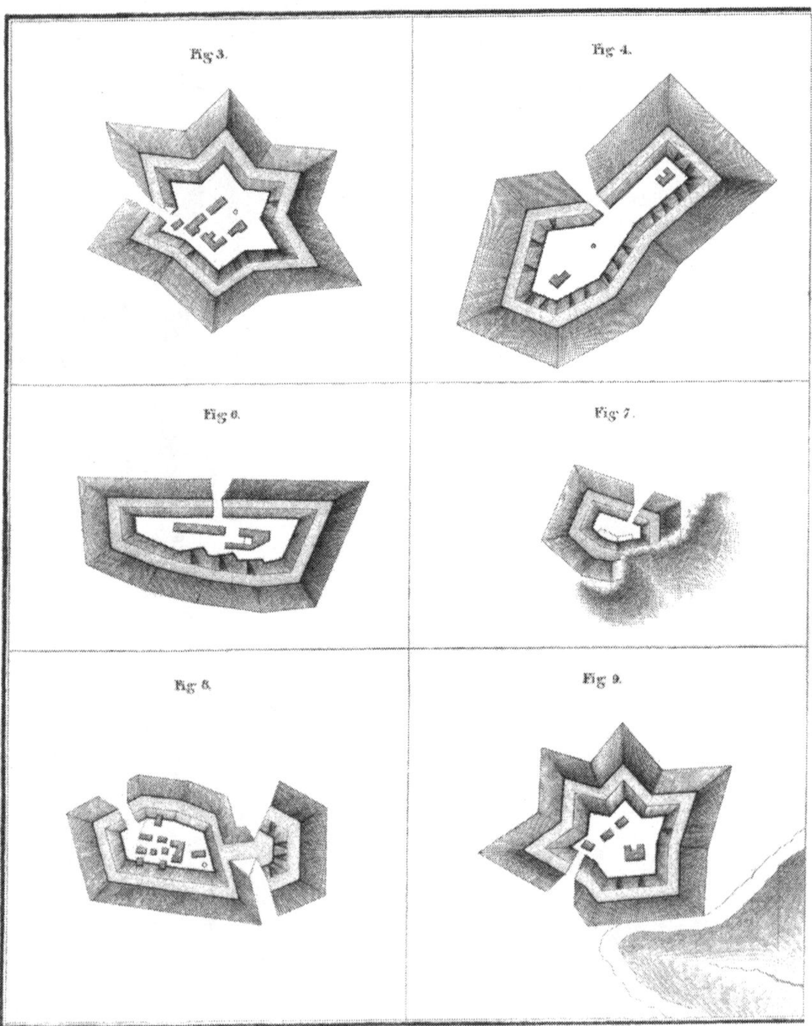

George [illegible] Lieut. Royal Engineers.

Fig 5.

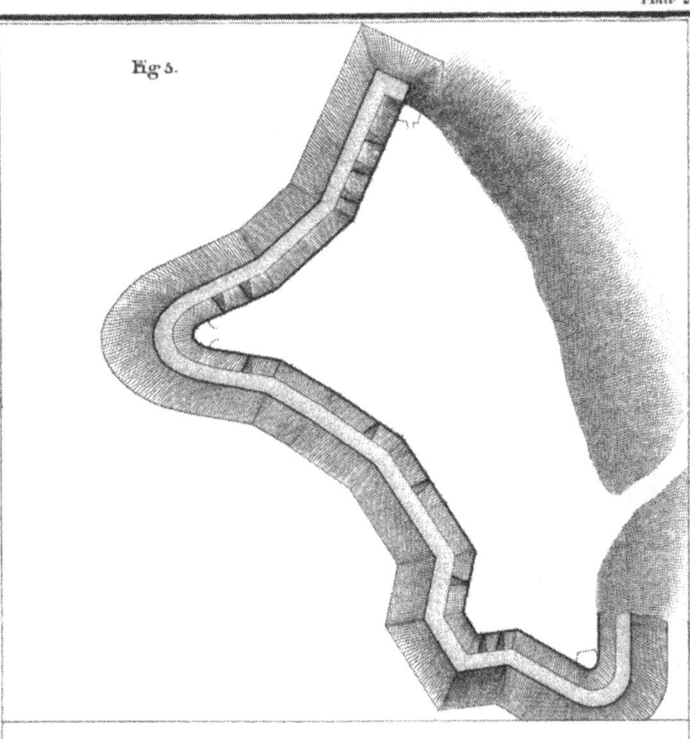

Fig 10.

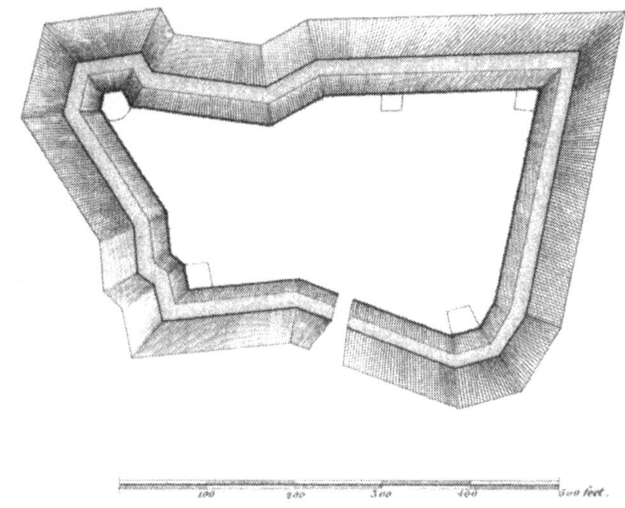

Plate 3.

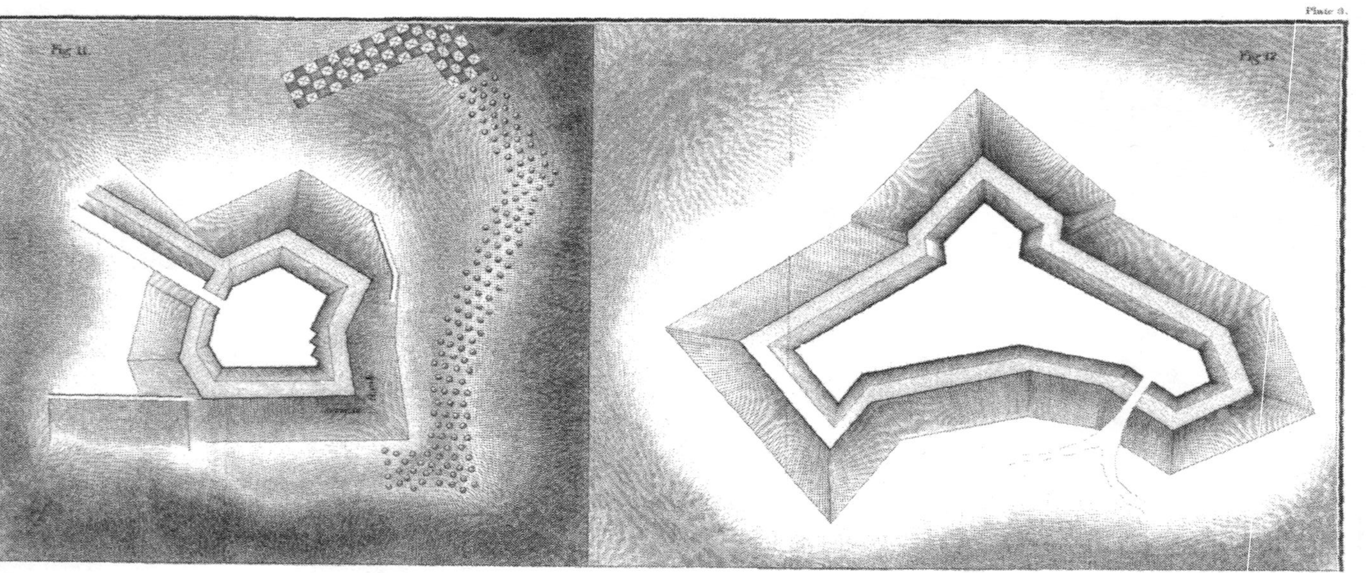

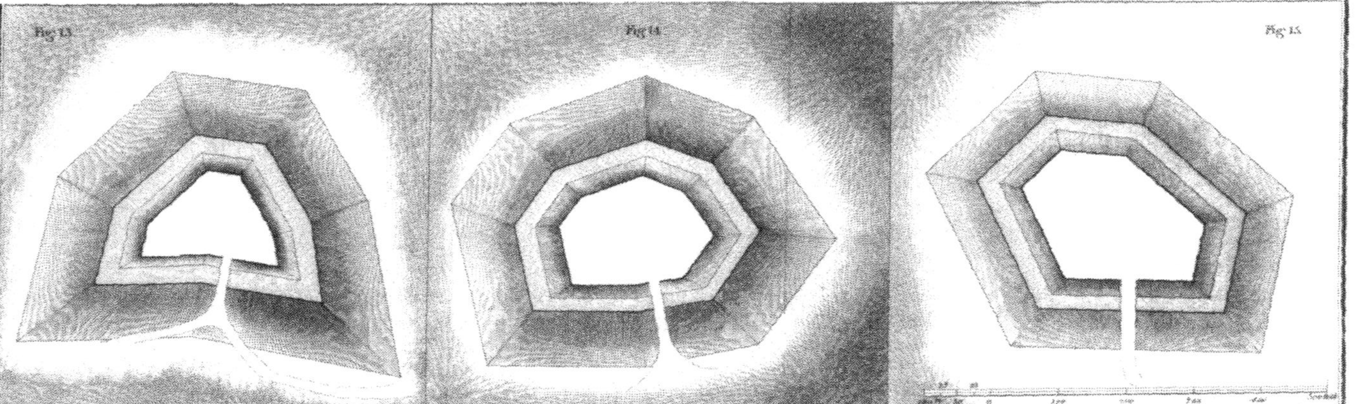
Fig. 13
Fig. 14
Fig. 15

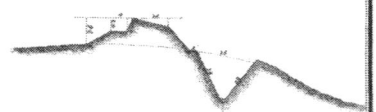

Fig 16.

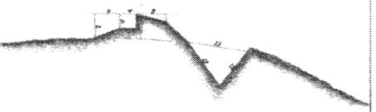

Fig 17.

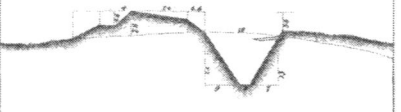

Fig 18.

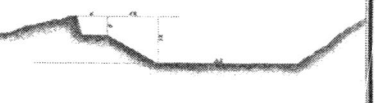

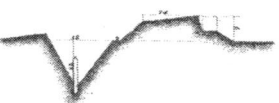

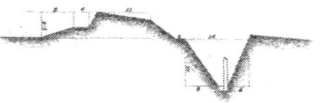

Fig 19.

Fig 20.

Fig 21.

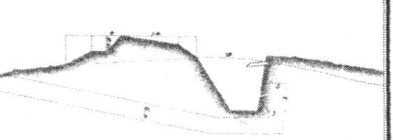

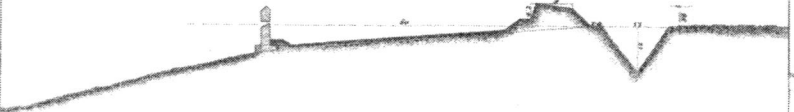

Fig 22.

90 feet.

Fig 23.

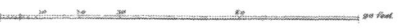

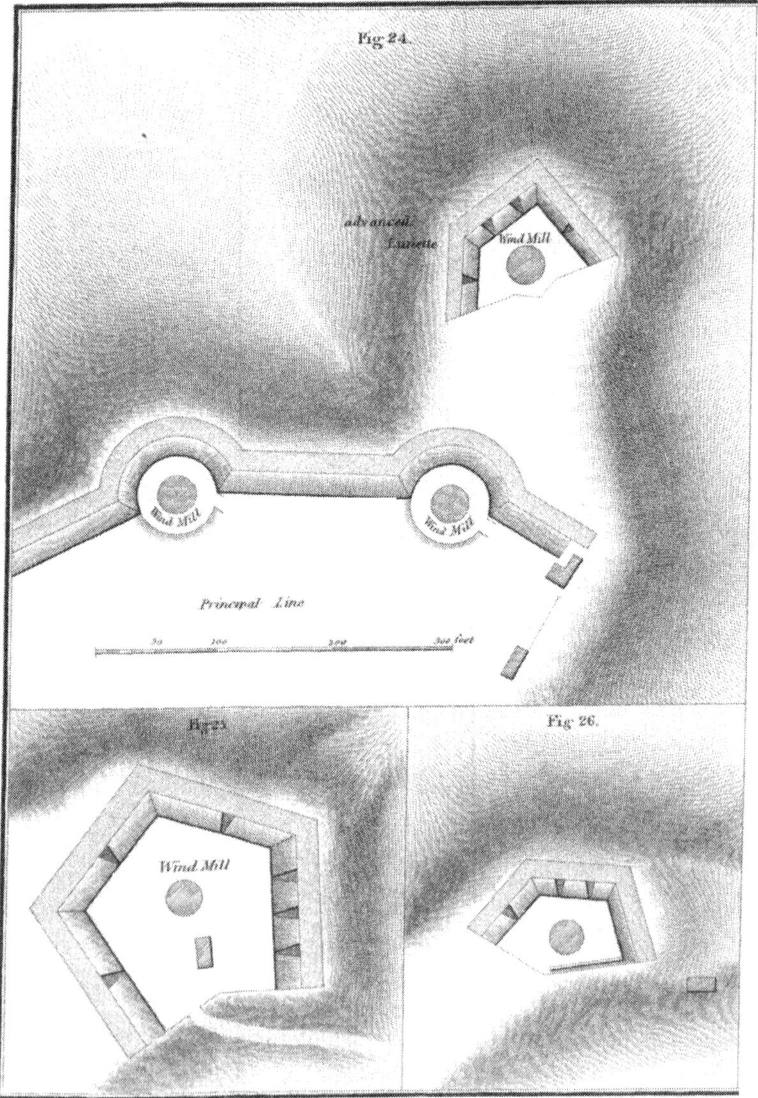

George Hotham Lieu.t Royal Engineers

Plate 5.

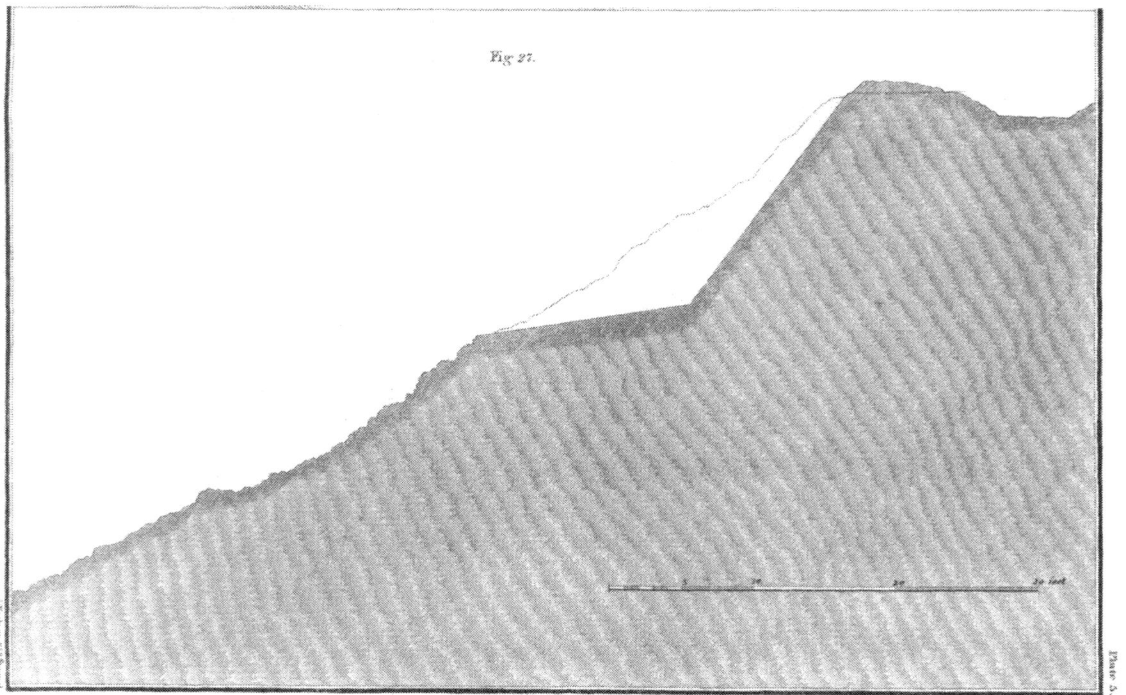

Fig 27.

J. Neele sc. 352 Strand

GROUND in front of LI

Converted into Lines by

LORD WELLINGTON

in 1810

Pa

Mil

Sit

0 3/4 1/2 1/4 0 1 2 3 4

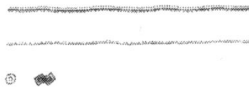

Scale of British statute Miles.

Engraved for Lt. Colonel John T. Jones of the Corps of Royal Engineers, 1818.

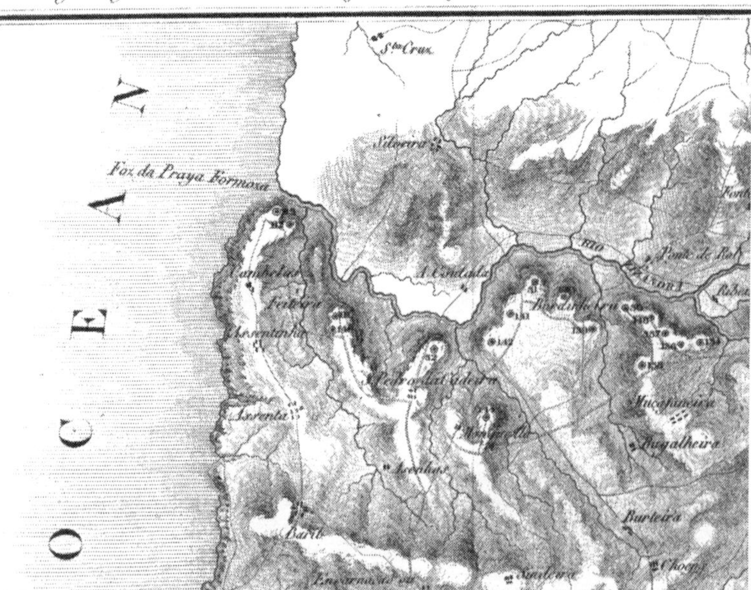

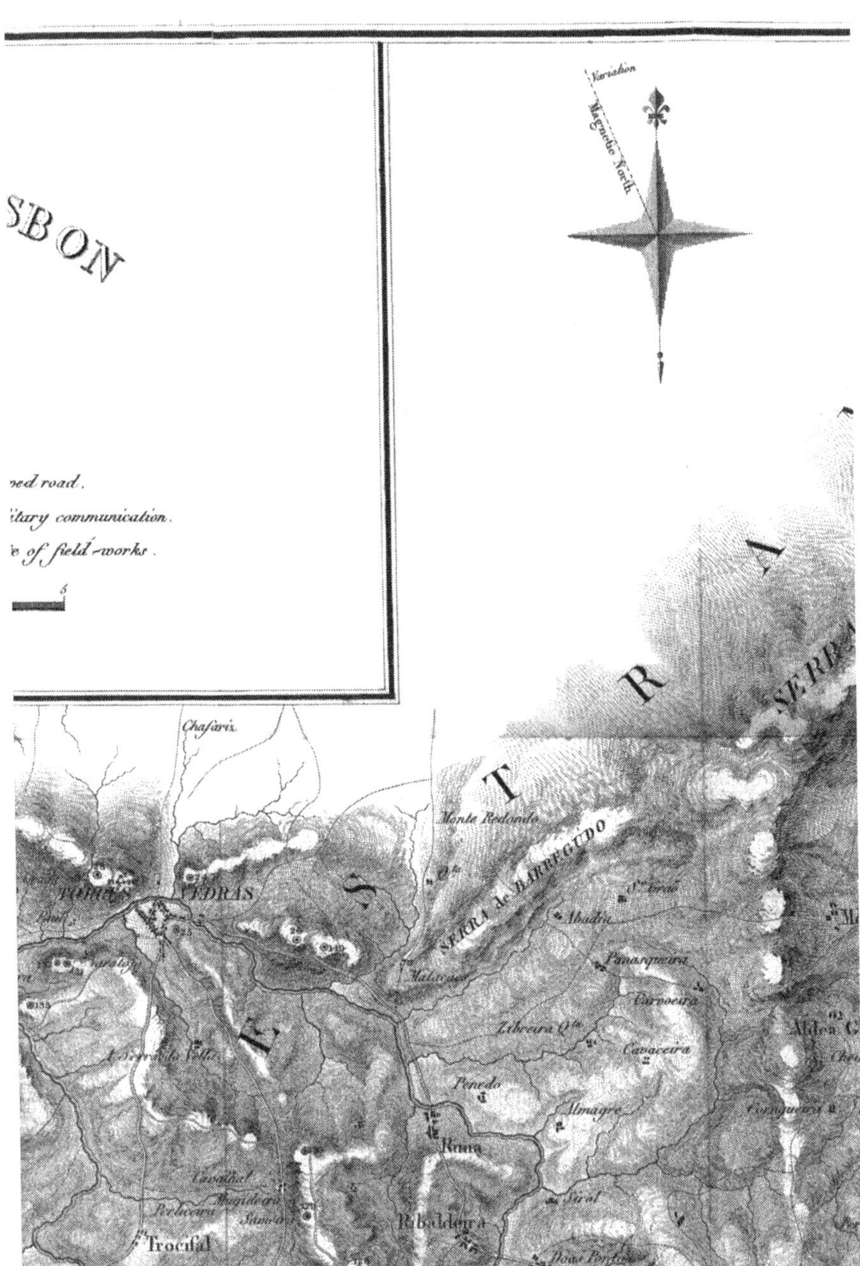

SBON
Variation
Magnetic North
ned road.
litary communication.
e of field-works.
Chafariz
Monte Redondo
SERRA de BARREGUDO
TORRES VEDRAS
Abadia
Matacaes
Carvoeira
Zibreira
Cabeceira
Penedo
Almagre
Runa
Ribaldeira
Trocifal
Sirol
Aldea

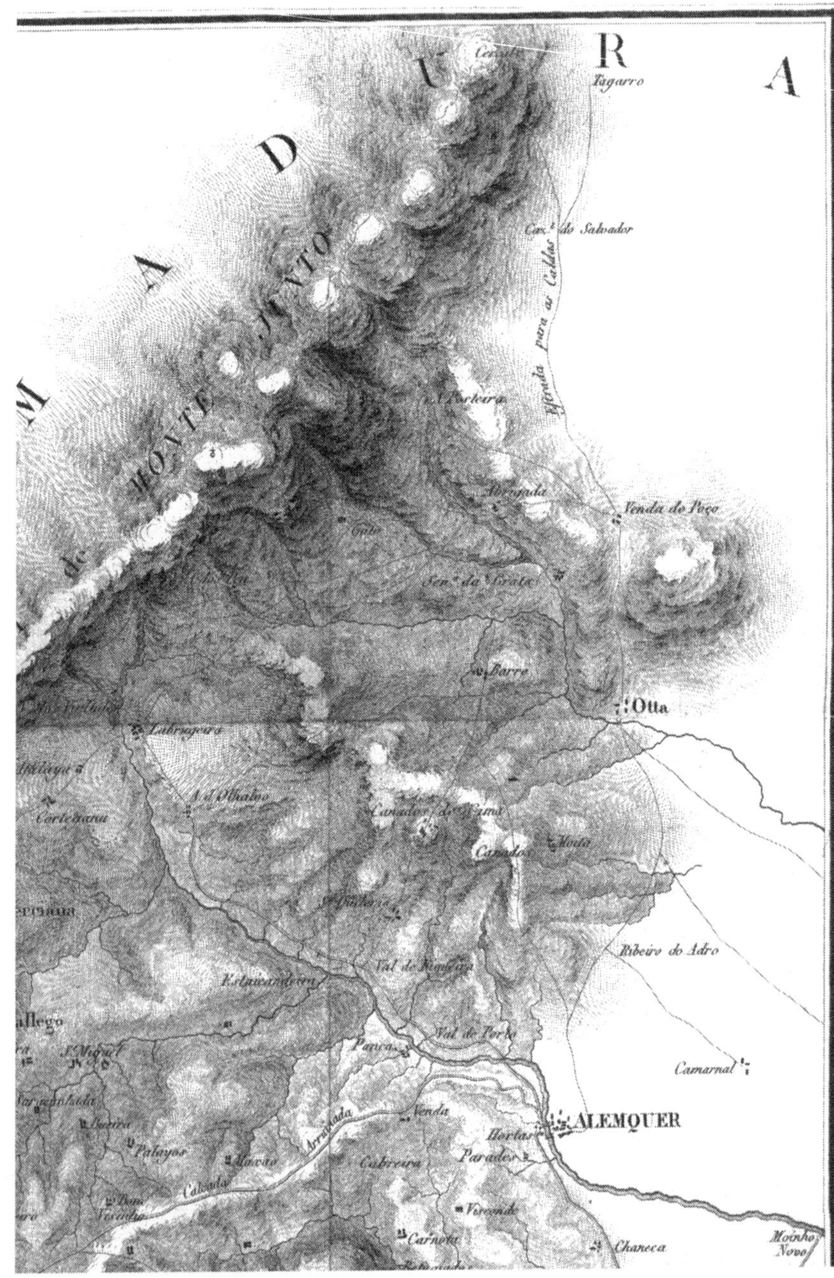

M A D U R A
MONTE JUNTO
Tagarro
Estrada para as Caldas
Venda do Poço
Otta
Ribeiro do Adro
Camarnal
ALEMQUER
Hortas
Paredes
Venda
Cabreira
Carnota
Chaneca
Moinho Novo
Val de Porto
Palayos

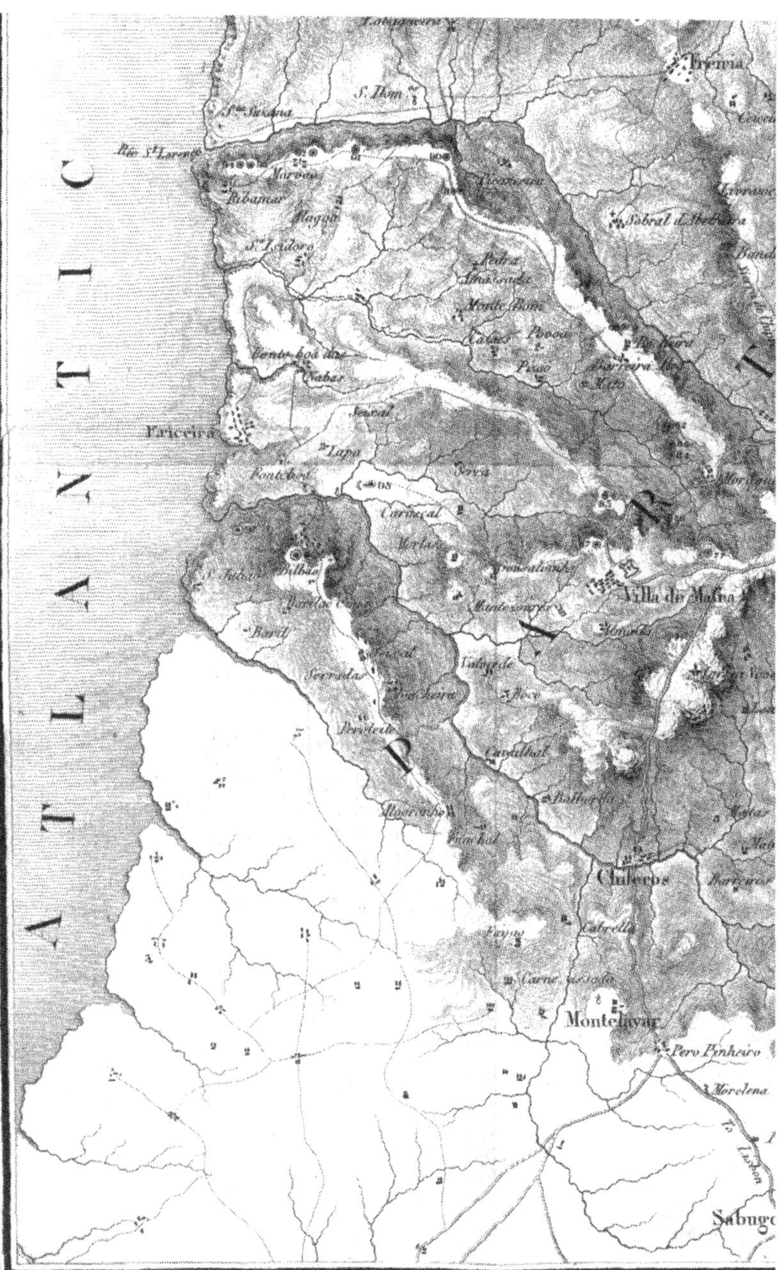

ATLANTIC
Ericeira
Villa de Mafra
Chileros
Montelavar
Pero Pinheiro
Morelena
Sabugo
To Lisbon
Sobral
Lapa
Cabrella
Carne assada

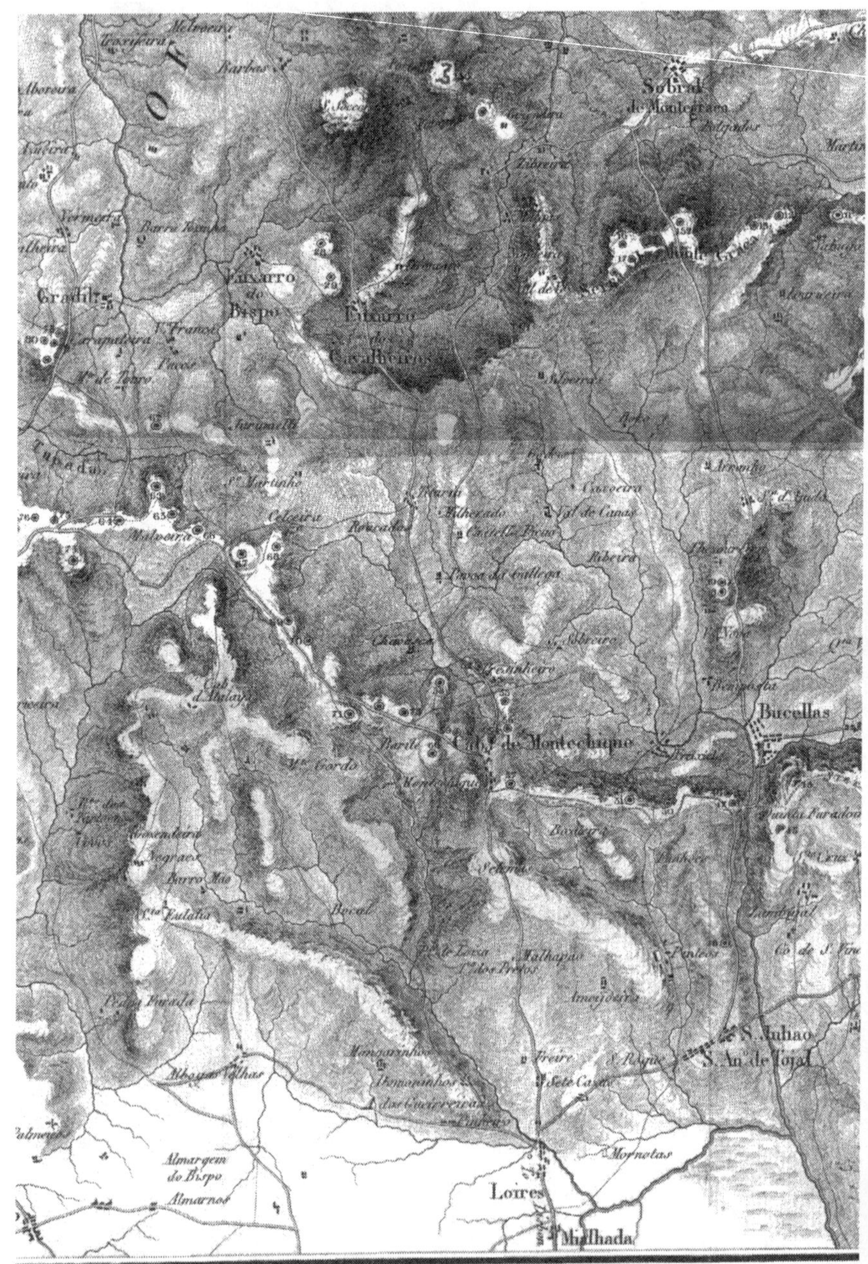
Sobral de Montegraça
Bucellas
Loires
Milhada
S. Julião
S. An. de Tojal
Gradil
Almargem do Bispo
Almarnos
Mornotas

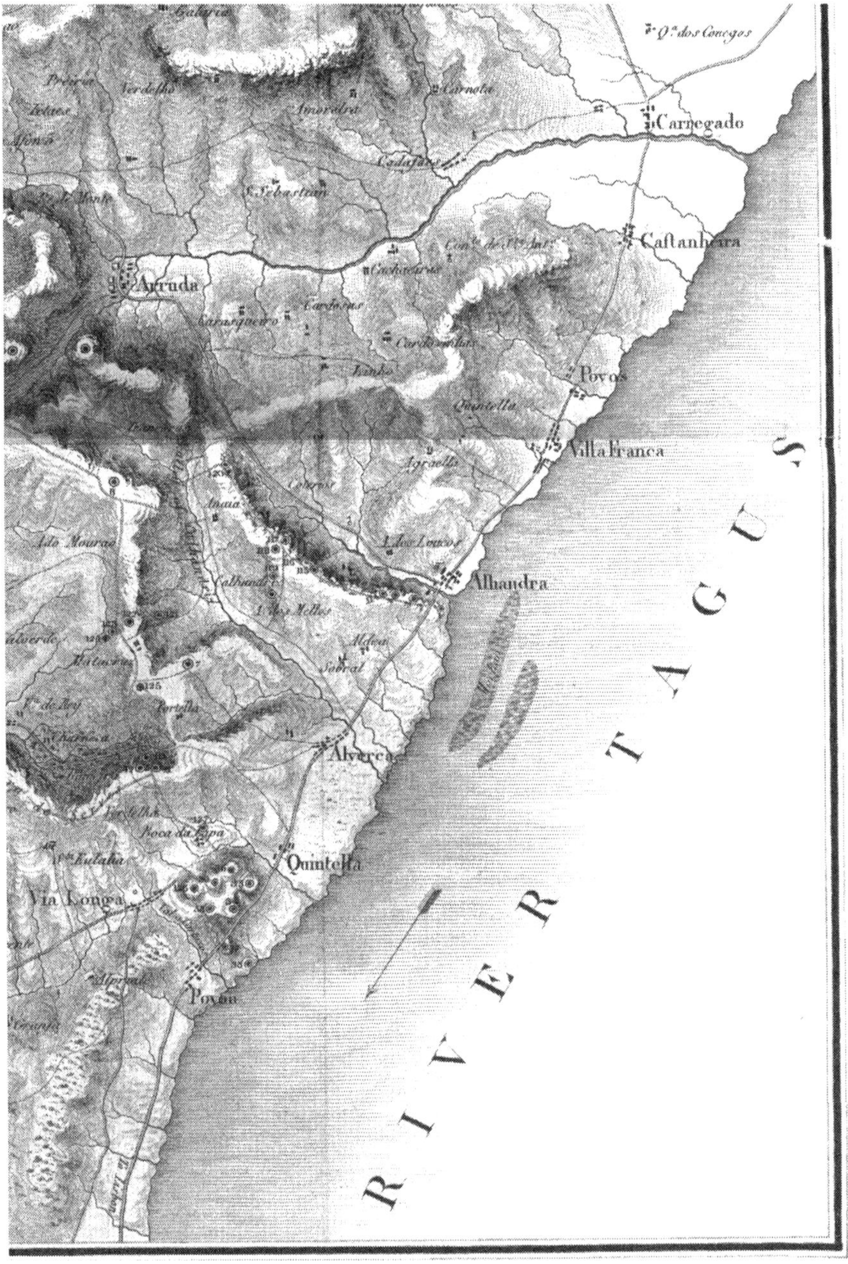

Qta dos Conegos

Carnota

Carnegado

Verdelha

Cadafaes

S. Sebastian

Castanheira

Arruda

Povos

Quintella

Villa Franca

Alhandra

Sobral

Alverca

Boca da Lapa

Quintella

Via Longa

Povoa

RIVER TAGUS

www.ingramcontent.com/pod-product-compliance
Lightning Source LLC
Chambersburg PA
CBHW030933150426
42812CB00064B/2825/J

* 9 7 8 1 8 4 7 3 4 4 6 3 2 *